8

THINGS TO KNOW ABOUT

Where We Go

Rainey Marie Highley

ISBN: 9798446355082

Sedona, Arizona
USA

TABLE OF CONTENTS

Where we had thought to find an abomination,

We shall find a god;

Where we had thought to slay another,

We shall slay ourselves;

Where we thought to travel outward,

We shall come to the center of our own existence;

Where we had thought to be alone,

We shall be with all the world.

-Joseph Campbell

DEDICATION

**THIS BOOK IS
DEDICATED TO MY MOTHER,**

LISA MARIE HIGHLEY

**WHOSE LAUGHTER, LOVE,
JOY, AND ANGELIC SUPPORT
RAIN DOWN ON ME
FROM ABOVE.**

I now see the Light everywhere—
in you as well as in me.

-The Afterlife of Billy Fingers

Introduction

The Pact

This book was written and coauthored by my mother, Lisa Marie Highley, but not during her time on Earth. She has lovingly helped me write this book from the other side; in a place we know as the Afterlife. Her love for me easily extends through space, time, the cosmos, beyond life and death, into an entirely new realm of truth, clarity, unconditional love, and never-ending joy beyond our wildest imagination. We know this realm quite well, for it is where we come from and where we shall return at the end of this Earthly life.

My mom was diagnosed with Stage 4 cancer five years before she transitioned. The one thing a terminal diagnosis gives family members is time to discuss the dying process and say proper goodbyes. Before my mom died, we sat down with my Aunt

Laura (my mom's sister and best friend in this world and beyond!), Laura's husband Al, my boyfriend John, and my mom's hospice nurse, Manny. On multiple occasions we discussed my mom's impending death and what would happen once she passed. We made a very clear agreement about how we would communicate after she transitioned to the other side.

Having written and published five books by the time of my mom's diagnosis, (two of them completely channeled) I was very familiar with communicating with our soul family on the other side of the veil. I knew in my heart of hearts that my mom was on her way to something absolutely spectacular. I even felt a tinge of jealousy. "I don't understand why you get to go first. I am the one who longs to return Home, not you," I pleaded.

Mom's sister, Laura, on the left, and Mom on the right.

It was true, my mom loved Earthly life. She engaged in the spectacle and drama of life with passion. She wanted <u>nothing</u> more than to be by the side of her sister Laura, me and my brother, Jeremy, and her grandkids, Zeya and Valyn, for a long, dramatic Earthly life. For me, it was much different. Pretty much from the first inkling of my awakening, I was gifted/cursed with a vivid memory of Home. I longed fully and *deeply* to return to my spiritual home. Everything about this Earthly experience felt off. *Something* wasn't right and I did not want to stick around long enough to find out exactly what it was. It wasn't fair that she got to go and I had to stay! *Why?*

I had tons of questions for Mom to answer as soon as she passed. Because of these questions, I asked (very clearly and in front of our witnesses), "Mom, when you die, you have to promise me that you will immediately, *immediately,* come to visit me and *tell me everything!*" I continued,

> I mean EVERYTHING! I *know* I can communicate with you; I *know* I will be able to hear you. Please let me know what the dying process is like, what death is like, and most importantly, what the HECK is going on here on Earth. Tell me who is responsible for poisoning our water supply and for laying chemtrails all over the planet!

People laugh about my chemtrail question because it seems so trivial compared to other real problems happening across the globe. However, I *knew* something was not right here on Earth and I had to find out what it was! How were massive human and animal-rights violations taking place worldwide without *any* assistance or intervention from a higher power or more advanced race?

And what about the Fermi Paradox? Why have we had ZERO contact with off-planet alien life? I mean real, in person meetings between humans and aliens? And how have no advanced alien races shown us a better way to live so we could avoid so much of our suffering? Somehow, I knew that if we could get to the bottom of who was responsible for flying the chemtrail airplanes all over the world to "modify Earth's weather," we would get to the bottom of all the big questions of our existence. *And I was right.*

My mom agreed and swore in front of Aunt Laura & Al, me & John, and Manny, (on several occasions) that she would come back to me IMMEDIATELY upon passing. This was our pact. It was a crystal-clear agreement made in front of our entire family. These two things I knew beyond a shadow of a doubt:

1. Mom would come and tell me everything, and
2. She would be my guardian angel for life.

This is a photo of my mom about six weeks before she passed. To the front left is Aunt Laura, to the right is my brother Jeremy. In the back to the left is Laura's husband Al and to his right is Mom's hospice nurse, Manny.

Mom was the most loyal person I knew. She always kept her word, *always*. I knew this would be no different. For several months before her death, Mom teetered between living and dying. Every single night from February to July 2018, I cried myself to sleep at night thinking this would be the night. It was such a stressful time. Even though I remembered Home, this was my first experience with human death and dying in this life.

One night on July 24, 2018, I found myself in the shower when I heard very clearly and loudly, *"Rain. Rain it's me. RAIN!"* I fell to my knees in tears. No one else called me *Rain.* No one. I knew she had died. I dried off, put on my robe, and ran to my office with a notebook and a pen. (It was important for our communication to be unobstructed by technology. For more, see the *Addendum: You Can Do It Too.*) *"I made it, Rain! I made it! I made it to the other side and I am SO HAPPY here!! I love it here!!"* I heard my mom as clear as if she were standing right in front of me. For the next several hours, she kept her promise. She came back and told me *every*thing.

On the pages that follow, I reveal her detailed message to me about the Afterlife, our life on Earth, the death and dying process, and what to expect when we drop these Earthly bodies. Most of what I learned from Mom left me feeling like an enormous weight had been lifted off my shoulders, freeing me to emerge into a whole new realm of existential living. It was such a feeling of relief and comfort that I literally cannot wait to share it with you!!

That said, the information she conveyed about the truth of what is happening on Earth has been quite difficult to digest. At the beginning, my mom just said, "It is way worse than you can even imagine. *But* it is also way better than you can imagine too." Just sitting with that revelation took some time. Once she taught me what was happening and why, it helped ease the pain and suffering of the Earth situation tremendously. I hope Mom's message provides you with an overwhelming sense of relief and clarity, just like it did for me.

Some of you have asked what people look like in the Afterlife. When my mom shows herself to me now, she usually looks like the image on this page—long, silky brown hair and the 20-something face and body she had here on Earth. She reminds me that in the Afterlife, you can present yourself anyway you like…anyway you can imagine. In the Afterlife, every single being is a shapeshifter. Everyone is easily capable of being anything they can imagine. Sometimes my mom reveals herself to me as a red cardinal, a dove, a butterfly, or a tiny, tiny green lizard. However, she reverts to her best Earthly version of herself most often when communicating with me. We will get into all the juicy details of the Afterlife in upcoming chapters, so I will leave it there for now.

As to voice, for those of you who knew my dear, sweet mother during her time on Earth, you may remember the way she talked or the way she laughed. I remember it too. I can hear her voice so clearly at times when we communicate. Often, however, she gifts me her response like a flower that opens as she hands it to me. It becomes my joy to translate her complete thought into our limited human vocabulary. Sometimes, though I try my best to keep this communication as pure as possible, my voice slips in. You may recognize its tone, or frequency.

I say all of this to let you know that I have received, retained, and communicated my mom's message in the purest way I know how. I have attempted to use words or phrases that she may have used or liked while on Earth. However, she is much more expansive now. She is her full, complete, higher self now. What we experienced of her on Earth was like meeting only the pinky toe of who she *really* is.

It brings me so much elation to communicate with my mom now. I would catch glimpses of her higher self during her time on Earth. I could see that beautiful, bright, angelic being that she was inside. From the kindness she showed to absolutely everyone, including complete strangers, to her willingness and strength to break a familial generational curse, to raising two amazing children (lol!), to making her close friends and loved ones laugh until they peed their pants, my mom allowed so much of her soul to shine through while she was alive. My mom was so much fun to be around.

Although I miss spending time with the Earthly-version of Mom, our relationship now is so much larger and more evolved. Experiencing my mom now, without an Ego-virus to contend with, is one of the sweetest experiences of my life! We get along perfectly! We sing together. We talk all the time. We cook together. We go on walks together. We listen to music together.

We play with puppies together. And now, we are writing a book together. *It is a dream come true.*

Mom is my guardian angel now and she is helping me so much from the other side. Because of her, I caught the cancer in my breast early. I found the perfect breast cancer surgeon because of my mom. I fell in love with my life partner, John, because of her. She had John hand deliver my sweet baby boy, Piper (my 4-year-old Pekingese), to me to be by my side throughout the entire breast cancer journey. She showed me how singing every single morning helped raise my vibration to keep the cancer cells from growing.

Mom gave me the wisdom to update and remodel my Sedona house so I could offer it as a sanctuary to visitors as a vacation rental property. This income gives me the freedom to do what I love and live wherever I want. My mom helped me with that. I am free, peaceful, abundant, and healthy because of her assistance. I am so grateful for all my mom has done for me both in this Earthly life and beyond. Most of all, I am profoundly grateful for the ongoing relationship I have with Mom despite living on opposite sides of the veil.

My mother reminds me that our bond and continuing love is not unique. In fact, many of you reading this book right now communicate in your own special way with a loved one who is now on the other side. You understand deeply, within your soul, what it means to watch someone you love to go through the death and dying process. May you experience waves of clarity, relief, and a peace that passes all conscious perception when reading this book.

It is my intention that every single person reading this book be gifted with an understanding and soul remembrance that forever changes your perspective and radically improves your life. May this shift be so huge in fact, that on the day of your transition, you will have the strength and confidence to face death with the heart of a warrior.

In the words of the late poet Mary Frye,

> Do not stand at my grave and weep;
> I am not there. I do not sleep.
> I am a thousand winds that blow.
> I am the diamond glints on snow.
> I am the sunlight on ripened grain.
> I am the gentle autumn rain.
> When you awaken in the morning's hush
> I am the swift uplifting rush
> Of quiet birds in circled flight.
> I am the soft stars that shine at night.
> Do not stand at my grave and cry;
> I am not there.
> I did not die.
>
> -*Do Not Stand at My Grave and Weep*, Mary Frye

My mom holding her arms out to catch me while diving at Uncle Mont & Aunt Gail's lake house.

Thank you, Mom,

for encouraging me to jump and be brave...

...and for always being there to catch me!

We were together. I forget the rest.

-Walt Whitman

CHAPTER 1

Do Not Fear Death and Dying

If you have read my book, *Soul Family—Discover Your Authentic Soul Tribe*, you will know that I was diagnosed with Stage 2 breast cancer one month after giving the eulogy at my mom's funeral. To say it was a kick in the gut is the understatement of the century. That said, I found it FAR less difficult to face my own possible impending death through a breast cancer diagnosis than it was to assist my mom through the death and dying process.

Flashes of the last six months of my mom's life still haunt me to this day. The sounds. The smells. Machines. Medicine. Memories

I wish I could erase. Visions I wish I could unsee. Trauma I wish I could shed. If you have been through it, you *know.* I was so, so worried about the extent of my mom's suffering. It was **all** I could think about. It was almost unbearable. I cried all of the time and could not even fathom taking care of myself like normal (eating healthy, working out, sleeping). Very little sleep, no food, lots of coffee, and no time for me defined my time as my mom's caretaker.

Losing a loved one is hard. It changes you forever. It does not matter how old, how sick, or how ready to go our dying loved ones are...the truth is, we are never ready to lose our closest companions to death. Regardless of what you believe or know about death and the Afterlife, it still hurts. There is a sense of loss accompanying the death of a loved one that is simply inescapable. I think it is important to acknowledge that death is never easy, no matter how much you know. Please do not ever feel weak for experiencing that pain. The pain of loss is an inevitable part of human life.

For anyone who has stood by the bedside of a dying loved one, there are sensations and memories you will never forget. Ever. Like the smell of urine and bodily fluids or when the nurse forgot to give her morphine and she started screaming bloody murder from the pain! From a caregiver perspective, it felt as if my entire insides were being ripped to shreds and there was not a single thing I could do.

However, it is not my intention to relive a brutal memory. Instead, for those of you who have been there, all I am saying is that I *get* you. Like, *for real*. In fact, the very first thing I asked my mom after she transitioned, was about the dying process. Specifically, I wondered if Mom regretted not arranging for and taking a "time of death" pill (legal in California at the time). What she told me gave me great hope and relieved the tension, anxiety, and trauma I was carrying surrounding her passing.

The Death and Dying Process

Mom, now looking back, do you wish you would have taken the time of death pill and avoided all the suffering at the end of your life?

Absolutely not, Rain! I *knew* that I did not want to immediately reincarnate. Instead, I wanted to stay on in the Earth experience in the position of a Guardian Angel over Laura, you and Jeremy, and my grandkids. Because of this, it was extremely important to me to go through the entire death and dying process before transitioning. This is not a terrible time of suffering as it may appear from the outside. From my perspective, the last six months of my life were absolutely wonderful. The dying process allowed me the opportunity to re-live my life. Not in the same way it had happened before, though. This time I was able to live my life perfectly, the way it was intended to be lived. My parents were loving, attentive and kind. My entire life was different. It was beautiful. By the time I actually did transition, I felt a sense of completion in relation to my experience on Earth.

The way you re-lived your life before death, does everyone have that opportunity?

It is unnecessary for many people. For example, it is not necessary for those who are immediately coming back into a new body to begin a new life. Or those who are completely moving away from the Earthly experience altogether. They are just ready to leave. However, it was different for me. My mission was very specific. I would move from life as Lisa Marie Highley, human being, to life as a Guardian Angel over my loved ones still on Earth. Many, many souls who pass over move into a Guardian Angel role until each one of their loved ones has transitioned.

Any soul moving from human being to Guardian Angel will experience a re-living of Earthly life perfectly prior to death. The reason for this experience is so that the Guardian Angel is prepared to guide and protect in the highest frequency possible after transitioning. This requires a quick and intense working through karma to clear the energetic pathway for this Guardian Angel. It is also so the frequency of a life perfectly lived is fresh to the Guardian Angel. It makes the Guardian Angels better guides, better helpers, better manifesters, better protectors, and overall, better caretakers.

That is fascinating, Mom. I could never have imagined you were in a positive place while you were dying!

"Dying" sounds so dramatic! Can we choose a new word?

OMG Mom, it was *completely* dramatic and also completely *traumatic*!

My hope is that it will never be traumatic for anyone reading this book. I am so sorry you went through such trauma, Rain. Now that you *know* I was not in *any* pain throughout the process, does it make it less traumatic for you, honey?

It does, thank you. But what about when the nurse missed your morphine and you were screaming in pain?

Gosh, I know that seemed awful and must have been traumatic to observe. Just know that the human body protects itself from extreme pain. This is why some people pass out and lose consciousness. My body was in pain, yes, but I was protected from most of it. I encourage you and anyone else who has observed someone dying, to let go of any pain you believe you witnessed. Passing over to the Afterlife is an extremely joyful process. I would do it again and again and again. It was 100% the best part of my life!

Even better than having kids, lol?

Just *barely*, Rain. Lol!

What advice would you give to those of us still alive on how we can prepare for the death and dying process?

Stop all preparation, now! It is unnecessary. There is NOTHING to fear in the death and dying process. It may appear to those looking in on you as you go through the process that you are suffering. In fact, death and dying was a completely pleasurable process. Stop worrying about death, now!! There is nothing to fear! A moment spent worrying about death is a complete waste of energy.

I spent so much of my life worrying. In fact, it was such a waste of my life! I would recommend to anyone reading this book now, *Stop worrying about death and dying. There is no pain in death. There is nothing to fear!* All fear is a complete and total waste of lifeforce energy. I hope this message comes as a huge relief to caretakers of sick and dying loved ones everywhere. Please remember, it looks way worse from the outside!

That is such a relief, Mom! Step by step, take us through exactly what happens when you die.

The length of the dying process is determined by whether you are immediately reincarnating, staying on as a Guardian Angel, or moving on to something different. For those immediately reincarnating, the dying process may be much quicker. As I mentioned, for anyone staying on in the capacity of a Guardian Angel for their loved ones, a longer dying process is typically required.

Step One: Light

What happens when you first transition? Do you see light at the end of the tunnel?

For me, there was no tunnel. I saw light EVERYWHERE. I saw it and felt it right away. It was instantaneous. It was the most beautiful, expansive, all-encompassing, all-loving, magical LIGHT you can imagine. It was really unlike anything you experience on Earth. Going *into* the Light and becoming one with the Light was the very first thing that I noticed. I felt transformed by the presence of the Light. I felt at one with the Light. I did not want to leave. I did not want to return to Earth. I was so perfectly happy and content in the Light.

Do you stay with the Light or do you have to leave it?

I was so relieved to discover that the experience of joining with Light in oneness is something you can experience over and over and over and over again.

Was it a visual sensation?

Yes, and at least a million other sensations too! As you enter into the Light, you are flooded with sensation after sensation. In fact, it feels like tidal wave after tidal wave of the most wonderful, indescribable sensations are washing over your soul. Just experiencing Light itself from a million different perspectives is awe-inspiring!

LET YOUR SOUL STAND COOL AND COMPOSED BEFORE A MILLION UNIVERSES.

-WALT WHITMAN

Step Two: Flood of Sensation

What kind of sensation?

More sensations than you could ever imagine! It is the most wonderful, euphoric, beyond-description combination of feelings and sensations in existence. It is unlike anything on Earth!

Is this the best part of dying?

Rain, we *have to* change the vocabulary around death and dying. It is so morose!

Ok, so what is the best part about transitioning to utopia?

Funny, Rain! The truth is this tidal wave of sensation is literally one of the very *best* and most *amazing* things in existence! You are all going to LOVE passing over! It feels so great that most people want to experience the whole thing again.

Really? Wow! That is so hard to comprehend. After a lifetime of indoctrination about death being so scary and horrible!

Yes, the truth is <u>much</u> better!

Step Three: Self Awareness

Ok, so after this flood of amazingness, what happens?

I know I have said this before but remember that all of this happens at one time, in a moment, outside of time. So, it is not linear time like on Earth.

Just go with me here, Mom.

Ok, the next thing that happens is you have a moment of intimate self-awareness.

You mean you remember who you are?

Exactly. This is where all the "memories" of the Afterlife come washing over you like ocean waves. You become intimately aware of who you are, and your place among All That Is. You remember everything that you "forgot" while you were on Earth.

Step Four: Soul Family Reunion

What happens after you remember everything you were forced to forget on Earth?

As these incredible waves of sensation are washing over you, you are greeted by your loved ones, Guardian angels, ancestors, relatives, and friends on the other side. We call this your Soul Family. Just like you talk about in your book, *Soul Family—Discover Your Authentic Soul Tribe.*

Is this similar to our Earthly families?

No, Rain, it is much different. No matter how much you love your family on Earth, your Soul Family is a connection that extends beyond time, space, and external conditions. Your Soul Family is forever. It always was and always will be. Often, Soul Family members incarnate as family members on Earth.

So, basically a bunch of people greet you? Lol.

It is more than that. It is usually a HUGE party! Like a celebration beyond your wildest dreams. As soon as you gain Self Awareness (awareness of what has happened and who you *really* are), you are greeted by every single loved one who transitioned before you. They will appear to you in their optimum human form but will show you flashes of how they looked when you were on Earth together. It is a wonderful, beautiful, welcoming feeling unlike anything you have ever experienced in human body. They shower you with unconditional love and feelings of warmth and overwhelming joy. It is like being constantly showered with more love than you have ever known. The entire Soul Family Reunion is a million times more amazing than *anything* you have ever experienced on Earth.

Do Pets Go to Heaven?

What about our beloved pets? Do all pets really go to heaven?

One million percent YES! All beloved dogs, cats, fish, hamsters, ferrets, birds, you name it! They are all there with you in the Afterlife.

As you look around at your extremely large Soul Family, you recognize people you had forgotten about while on Earth; people you love deeply and unconditionally. It is a wonderful reunion! As you continue to gain awareness of your surroundings, you begin to notice every single beloved pet you have ever owned/loved/cared for, surrounding you. All the animals surrounding you are happy, healthy, playful, and in absolute bliss. It is so comforting to see and to know that everyone is fine and that no one ever actually "died." Seeing all of the animals I loved while on Earth was my favorite reunion of all time, Rain!

Do our pets always stay our pets?

All beings are completely free to experience existence however they wish. Just like all of us, pets are free to shapeshift and move between forms. It is such an incredible experience when you remember that your pets are actually your relatives and family members in other lives!

Step Five: The Life Review

What happens after the Soul Family Reunion?

Following the Soul Family Reunion, you are taken to your Life Review which no one attends but you.

Wait, wait, wait—*really? No one?*

That is right. Only <u>**you**</u> review your life. There is no judgment or punishment...no judge or jury handing out penalties for sins.

But I have heard that the Life Review occurs with a Council present?

That is only if the person having the Life Review requests it.

What would be a reason that someone would request a Council to be present at their Life Review?

If the individual was a member of a Council in the Afterlife, they may want to re-connect with the other Council members upon review of their Earthly life. It is entirely optional, however. No one must share their Life Review with anyone else. We know that Truth is a perspective, and your perspective is always your Truth. We honor every individual's Truth in the Afterlife.

Another reason an individual may request a Council present at Life Review would be if they are seeking advice or guidance on how to improve their conscious awareness in their next incarnation.

Did you request a Council at your Life Review?

No, Rain, I did not. I have had *many* incarnations and Life Reviews, so I knew what to expect. I went through my Life Review by myself and it was extremely eye-opening.

What do you mean, Mom?

No matter how wise or evolved you believe yourself to be on Earth, I promise that absolutely every single one of you will be horrified as you observe certain moments in your Life Review. You will think, "How could I have been so *unconscious?"* You will wonder why you felt it necessary to cause so much pain. Certainly, you will each experience varying degrees of sadness, regret, elation, and satisfaction as you witness the choices you made while on Earth.

During your Life Review, you will see how every decision in your Earthly life impacted others. You will observe the experience from the perspective of those you impacted. For me, this was extremely brutal. I witnessed, in gut-wrenching detail, the pain my actions and words had on my loved ones at various times in my life, including you and Jeremy. I watched in horror and instantly felt regret. I wish I could erase those moments and just make them go away. I was a silly, stupid human who let her ego get in the way.

So, would you say you felt sad after your Life Review?

Not sad in the way you experience sadness on Earth. However, I felt regret for certain decisions I made at various times in my life. I wish I could take the pain away from those I hurt. The Life Review caused me many feelings of sadness and regret. I felt empathy for the journey of others as I became aware of their unique perspectives and subsequent struggles.

Step Six: Entry into Next Role

What happens next after the Life Review?

Many people, especially those with a painful Life Review like mine, choose to *immediately* re-enter Earth and move into their next life incarnation. The intention is to live a better life, not make the same mistakes, and have a greater, more positive impact on one's environment.

Because of the pact you and I made before my passing, and because it would mean more to me to be by the side of my loved ones still on Earth throughout the remainder of their lifetimes, I chose to act in the role of a Guardian Angel. This means you can call on me for assistance at any time, Rain. Just say my name and ask for help.

Now there are those with absolutely exquisite Life Reviews who choose to act in a Guardian Angel role to assist children or loved ones they have left behind. One of the nice things about the role of Guardian Angel is that you are not limited to helping the people you chose to be a Guardian Angel for, you may also help anyone else who asks for help from Earth.

Guardian Angels

You mean that because you are now in the role of a Guardian Angel that any being on Earth may request your help?

Yes. However, there must be energetic resonance to even hear the request. So, we do not assist with negative or low-vibrational requests.

That makes sense. So, what you are saying is that someone reading this book right now could ask you for help?

That is right, Rain. I looooooooooove being a Guardian Angel! I love helping humans and animals whenever I can!

Is resonance the only requirement to get a Guardian Angel to help you?

In addition to purity of intention (vibrational resonance), it is best for the person to say my name out loud and what they need help with. So, like you say, Rain, *"Lisa Marie Highley please help me, Piper, Pee Wee, and Penelope right now!"* Situations where you say my name or wear my jewelry/clothing make it easier for me to intervene on your behalf.

What if we are too upset to think of anybody's name or to say anything out loud?

Luckily, all that is required of you to receive assistance from a Guardian Angel is that you ask for help. Saying, "HELP," out loud is enough. Sometimes just *thinking,* "Please help me," is enough. In times where no specific Guardian Angel is named, but help is requested, *any* Guardian Angel can come to your aid. Guardian Angels may assist anybody who asks.

Do you *have* to go help someone if they ask for you?

Never. As Guardian Angels, we have complete autonomy. We decide if and when we want to help souls on Earth. To be clear, no one is making us do anything. Everything is voluntary.

What happens next for Guardian Angels?

After a bit of time in "recovery and relaxation" following death, Guardian Angels begin a very intense, but very fun, training period. We learn from other Guardian Angels on the best way to assist and communicate. We also look deeply into the lives of our loved ones to see pain points where we can assist. Then we get to work! We can be with all of our loved ones at once and so we choose to always be with you. To be by your side, every single moment for the rest of your life!

Advice to Caregivers

What advice would you give to caregivers who are tending to a loved one who is dying?

This is an important question, Rain, because not only are the Baby Boomers facing their own mortality, but so many more people of all ages are falling victim to the increased toxicity of the environment around them. Death rates are on the rise. It is an important question for every single person reading this book. One day, each of you will face the death of a loved one. That is an unavoidable part of this Earth experience.

♥ My first piece of advice would be to stop judging yourself and stop criticizing what you have done or not done. I can *promise* you that once a person passes over to the other side, they completely drop all feelings of sadness, disappointment, and regret. They feel 100% total gratitude towards everyone who has loved them, and they feel total and complete forgiveness towards everyone. All grudges are completely dropped. All hostility is released. Everything, and I mean *everything*, in the past is forgiven and almost totally forgotten! Please don't waste one second thinking about what you could have done differently or better. We really are not thinking that way and we just want you to love yourself and forgive yourself!

♥ So, my advice to caregivers is to begin by LETTING GO. Let go of all criticism, all regret, all worry that you could have done something differently or something better...just let. It. Go. Now. Trust me, once you pass over you do not feel any judgment or criticism. All we remember are the good times. Please try and only focus on the positive memories.

♥ Next, I would suggest letting go of timing related to your loved one's transition. The exact time of death/passing is decided by the soul leaving the Earth body. You can try and keep them comfortable until they drop this Earth body, but you have zero influence on the time of death. So please let go of all worry and concern related to timing.

♥ Finally, remember it is not as bad as it seems. Every moment that our physical body gets weaker here on Earth, our light body is strengthening on the other side. Yin and yang. Our lifeforce energy is moving to the other side. Know that it is a beautiful, wonderful process and not something to be feared. Do your best to let your loved one go and try not to hold them here unnecessarily. As caretakers, one is really a steward, or a midwife, assisting with the re-birthing of a soul into the Afterlife. Even better, you can be happy for your loved one who has transitioned now that you know they are free of all pain and living in complete joy!

What can caretakers do to make the transition of a loved one easier?

Do your best to not unnecessarily extend the dying process on Earth. ***Let your loved one go.*** Hundreds of billions of dollars of healthcare money goes towards extending the life of a loved one by a few months, weeks, or days. Everyone says they want to die at home and yet the majority die in a hospital bed. Doing your best to release your fear surrounding death is one of the best things you can do for a loved one who is dying. Everyone has an appointed time of death. If it is their time, it is their time. There is nothing you can do to change it. So, try and let go. Release your loved one into the Afterlife with confidence and courage.

I think as a caretaker, it can feel like a personal failure when your loved one transitions because you were trying absolutely everything in your power keep them alive and ultimately, you failed.

Do your best to let go of that type of thinking, Rain. The goal of a caretaker is not to extend the life of their loved one. Let us be very clear about that. It is not your responsibility, nor do you have the ability, to extend another person's life. Try and get that out of your head. As a caretaker your responsibility is to act as a midwife for the transition of one's soul.

Death isn't as serious as it seems and we *will* meet again.

-The Afterlife of Billy Fingers

How do we best act in this capacity?

- First, let go of all fear of death.

- Second, let go of all attempts to extend the life of your loved one.

- Third, make every effort to make your loved one as comfortable as possible.

- Fourth, listen, do not talk. Please do not try to impart any wisdom about transitioning. Allow the loved one who is transitioning to have her own unique experience. Sit with them. Just be quiet with them.

- Fifth, in a perfect world you would hold a space of joy for your loved one. This is very challenging when dealing with human emotions. However, this is the ultimate goal of assisting a loved one with the transition of their soul into the Afterlife—to provide a calm, pleasant atmosphere for the transition of the soul out of Earth.

Mom, what would you say to individuals who have lost loved ones...husbands, wives, children? What advice would you give them?

I understand how challenging it is to experience what feels like great loss as a human being. Just know that the truth is that your loved one is not really dead. They are as alive as they have ever been. They are happier and more expansive than you have ever known them. Take the very best memory you have and amplify it times a million. That is the who they are now. The person you experienced on EARTH was only a small piece of their soul. Who they REALLY are is so much bigger than what you remember. So, give them the space to be much bigger than the person you knew.

Once you allow for the evolved expression of their soul, you may welcome them into your life as a guardian angel. This means that you verbally invite them into your life, each and every day. Ask for their help. Talk to them. Your loved one is still by their side just like on Earth, you just can't see them. Any time you say their name out loud, they will be there for you. So, say their name. Talk to them like you used to. Practice the art of intuitive listening. You will begin to hear them talking back to you.

Also, I would encourage you to do your best to pull yourself out of grief. Intuitive listening only works if your vibration is high. There really is no reason to be sad. You should be happy for your loved one because they are a million times better than they were on EARTH. Although there is sadness that you will not communicate the same way as you used to while they lived on EARTH, there is satisfaction in knowing that now you have a badass guardian angel by your side for the rest of your life. Your loved one is a zillion times more powerful and influential than they were on EARTH. And now you have them by your side at all times if you choose!

But don't our loved ones get tired of helping us all the time? I don't want to subject them to a life sentence of having to stay by my side when they could be out having the time of their lives in the Afterlife?

That is thoughtful of you to say, Rain. It does not inhibit our enjoyment of the Afterlife, **at all.** We can be everywhere all at once if we choose. Helping our loved ones is a great piece of joy in our lives. We are honored to assist you! There are no limitations in our assistance other than the rules of the game.

Here lies one
whose name was
written in water.

-John Keats

CHAPTER 2

The Afterlife is Better Than Imagined

Ok Mom, so what does it feel like when you die?

When you pass over, a HUGE WAVE of unconditional love sweeps over you. It is so overwhelming...so joyful....so GOOD in a way the human language cannot describe. A tidal wave of relief flows through you—through every molecule of your being—like a complete body, mind, and spirit cleanse. You feel truly born again!

It feels like waking from the scariest, most stressful nightmare you can imagine and then discovering you are really in paradise—clear blue ocean, waves crashing, dolphins splashing, bright sunshine—you are on the beach, waking from a nap. It was only a bad dream. Now you are back. You are Home.

Immediately after the huge wave of relief crashes over you, you begin to breathe for the very first time. You immediately realize that your entirely Earthly life was devoid of breath and littered with extremely strong delusions of separation. "Oh, thank God, it was all just a dream! Oh my God, this is what it feels like to really breathe! Wow. It feels so good to be HOME. It feels like I have been gone for so long!" Waves of elation, laughter, clarity, knowing, and truth sweep over you like powerful ocean waves knocking you down each time. It takes a moment to adjust again to feeling wonderful after feeling less than ok for a lifetime on Earth. It is a moment you will want to relish. A moment of being enveloped in the brightest, most wonderfully warm, and loving light you could ever imagine.

What do you look like when you die?

You experience a self-awareness unlike anything you have known in physical body. You instantly know you are dead. You know you have not one body, but can shapeshift between "looks," as I like to call them. So, when I looked at myself, I was a bright, shining light but I was also the body of Lisa Marie Highley, as I had been on Earth. However, I did not look anything like I did when I was dying. Instead, I appear like I looked when I was 22 years old. Perfect. Youthful. Glowing. Fresh, tan skin. Thin body. Long, shiny hair.

It was such a RELIEF to know how I *really* looked, on the inside, after aging into my late sixties on Earth. I was overjoyed to know that my soul was still beautiful, although my Earthly body was not when I transitioned. *Remember how I told you Rain, that it was what was on the inside that truly matters? Remember how I told you that it was the soul inside of you that really counts?*

Well, I was right! Your earthly body does not matter one iota! It was just a vehicle you drove while on Earth. That was it! An avatar, nothing more. It was an amazing, unbelievable moment to feel beautiful, and to know that my soul was always beautiful, and the Earth experience was only an illusion.

You mean because you went through the aging process while on Earth?

Exactly. It was such a relief to drop my 68-year-old, cancer-ridden body and trade it in permanently for a beautiful, younger model! Lol! Now keep in mind, you can transition into any form you desire in the blink of an eye. Often, people revert to light body as their "default form" in the Afterlife. However, immediately upon transitioning or when greeting loved ones who have passed, many souls revert to their human forms. It is considered natural to remain visually connected to one's former life. Once the soul becomes acclimated to "real life" as we call it, the need for Earthly identification becomes less important. You will be able to look any way you choose, but at the same time, you will identify so much stronger with unseen things. Your appearance is of little importance in the Afterlife.

Daily Life in the Afterlife

Mom, can you give me an idea of what daily life is like in the Afterlife?

The first major difference between Earth and the Afterlife is that we do not experience time like you do on Earth. In fact, we do not experience time at all. So, the whole concept of "daily life" does not really apply. For example, we do not have sunrise, then daytime, then sunset, and then night. We move between whatever we would like to experience for as long as we like. Each being experiences "life" differently. Another huge difference you will notice is that individual lives are not impacted by collective decisions like they are on Earth. There is no weather to contend with or traffic or political upheaval or social unrest. Life is peaceful and amazing all the time!

You mean you do not have to follow rules in the Afterlife?

Not many, Rain. The Afterlife is all about *freedom.* You can live your life any way you like because no one else is impacted by your decisions. It is a win-win for everyone! You get to do absolutely anything you want and no one gets hurt!

Can you give me an example?

Sure! If you want to experience a day like you had on Earth, where you worked all day, ate meals and went to bed at night, you absolutely *could* have that experience. However, working for survival is completely unnecessary. Every single being in existence has absolutely every single thing they could ever want or need. Everything is available to everyone. No one is harmed. Every being is safe. That is the biggest difference between the Afterlife and Earth. It seems small but that one difference changes absolutely everything.

Imagine, Rain, what life would be like if you never had to worry for your safety or the safety of your loved ones. No one will get sick and die. No one deteriorates. There is no pain! Everyone is safe. Everyone is healthy, in every moment. Imagine not having to eat to survive. Not needing money. Having anything and everything you could ever imagine in every single moment. The only limitations you experience are the limitations of your own imagination.

**The visible world is
no longer a reality and
the unseen world
no longer a dream.**

-William Butler Yeats

Wow. It is just so much to digest. It feels so right in my heart and in my soul. I feel the truth of what you are saying but I have no conscious memory of it.

So basically, take the very best things about Earth and amplify those things by a million! THAT is the Afterlife!

Does the sun rise in your reality in the Afterlife, Mom?

Although there is no time in the Afterlife, most of us choose to experience sunrise and sunset. Where I am, the sun rises every day, Rain! I *love* watching the sun rise!

So, just to be clear, even though the Afterlife does not *normally* have sunrise, daytime, sunset and night, any one individual can have whatever they want?

That is right, Rain. The answer to your question is a bit more complex than you may think. Some worlds have certain weather conditions or abide by laws of physics, but you do not have to experience any weather other than your own. You can literally have a bubble of your own perfect weather around you at all times, completely unaffected by outside conditions.

That sounds amazing! What if you decide to visit a friend and they have stormy skies?

I can choose to enjoy their creation or I can have my own atmosphere follow me within their experience, without being affected by their choice of weather.

Are we like floating around on clouds and playing harps in white robes or what?

No, it is not like that at all! The Afterlife is relatable. It is like the Earth experience amplified by a million. All the most beautiful things on Earth are just one slight glimmer of insight into the Afterlife. For example, the rainbows you see are only a tiny sliver of what rainbows are REALLY like. Rainbows are alive, sentient beings that move in shapes and contain ALL the colors of the Macroverse (millions of new colors beyond the visible spectrum). Just being in the presence of a rainbow is life changing. Every single color they shine is healing and nurturing. You can incarnate as a rainbow and experience *being* all those different colors.

What about animals? Are there animals in the Afterlife?

Many animals on Earth are a tiny speck of what they really are like in the Afterlife. Common "animals" I see in the Afterlife? There are many dogs, cats, dolphins, whales, elephants, birds, butterflies, and even fireflies, in the Afterlife. However, they are much more expansive in the Afterlife. For example, there are countless varieties of birds. Imagine the brightest colored bird possible and amplify that times a million. The colors are outside of the human perspective and beyond anything you can imagine.

Some birds leave trails of beautiful rainbow art...like the complete opposite of a chemtrail. The bird trail rains down blessings and healing to anyone who passes underneath. On top of that, the bird trail releases the most incredible aroma you could ever imagine. The most delicious, mouth-watering fragrance loved by all. You could actually spend lifetimes just studying the birds alone.

Fascinating, Mom! Do people die in the Afterlife?

No, there is no killing, murder, death, or dying in the Afterlife. Every being is protected by a shield and cannot be harmed by another. There is no sickness, no sadness, and no suffering. There is an overwhelming degree of comfort, safety, and unlimited joy in the Afterlife.

Let me just say this. The very best you ever feel on Earth is not 1% of the positive, wonderful feelings you experience in the Afterlife. All of the seemingly "bad" things on Earth have already been worked through and successfully resolved in the Afterlife.

Is that why so many people here on Earth are on antidepressants?

Yes, even though the mind goes through a forgetting, the soul never forgets. Something inside of every person on the planet, remembers what it is like in the Afterlife. That is the innate disconnect everyone feels while in the Earth experience...a soul-level memory of where you are from and where you are going once you transition.

What types of activities do you engage in besides watching the sun rise?

I spend a lot of time with loved ones. We regularly get together for breakfast, cliffside overlooking the ocean!

Tell me about breakfast. Who does the cooking and cleaning?

This should be really great news for many souls out there...*no one* is doing the cooking and cleaning! There are no menial tasks in the Afterlife because you can create whatever you want in an instant, just by thinking about it. Unless someone specifically wants to have the experience of cooking and putting together a meal, meals are created through instantaneous thought. Of course, the act of eating is unnecessary for survival but so much fun for many. Plus, food is not harmful in any way in the Afterlife. It is pure fun.

What is the best part about breakfast in the Afterlife?

The coffee, Rain, the coffee...it is unlike anything you could EVER imagine! It is a high vibrational honey-like elixir that is so crystalline, so iridescent, so sparkly, and so nutritious that you will want to drink it all the time! It is extremely delicious and satisfying. It fills you up from the inside, making you feel the very best you have ever felt! When you feel this good, Rain, I promise, it is like every moment is a miraculous wonder!

Is the coffee why you choose to meet for breakfast?

That is exactly right, Rain! My closest friends, family, and loved ones join every morning to have breakfast on the patio by the ocean. We see lots of dolphins, whales and mer-people in the ocean! We like to go at sunrise when the sun is a million different colors and the day comes on slowly.

What do you do after breakfast?

After breakfast, I like to paint. I change my location every day. Sometimes I am on the roof of a castle, overlooking a beautiful kingdom. Sometimes I am in Africa on a safari, painting all of the animals I see. Sometimes I will choose to take lessons by someone famous, like Leonardo DaVinci or Monet. After my creative time, I will join friends to sing together. We all have beautiful voices so it is really fun to harmonize and come up with songs.

Are there famous people, like rock stars, in the Afterlife?

There are those recognized for their musical ingenuity and creativity, though every living soul is a skilled musician in their own right. We do go to concerts, in fact. Many musicians who were famous on Earth are also famous in the Afterlife. Creativity and Expression Celebrations are popular throughout the Macroverse. All are invited. All are welcome. None are excluded. All are loved. There is no hierarchy. Only individuals appreciated for their unique gifts and contributions.

Do you get bored in the Afterlife?

Never. Ever! If I have nothing else to do, I often tune into Earth to check in on my loved ones. I help wherever I can. Remember Rain, that in the Afterlife, I am able to do anything I want, anything I can imagine, at any time. How could I get bored?!!

Do you miss me and Jeremy?

Of course, Rain! But the truth is there is really no time for missing anyone because by the moment you think about them, they appear. That means that even though you are still on Earth, you and Jeremy are just moments away from being with me again, if that makes sense. It is a mere moment away.

Entertainment in the Afterlife

Is Earthly entertainment something we will miss on the other side?

The Afterlife lacks nothing. You will not miss anything about Earth. In fact, there are those who will choose not to remember anything. Earthly entertainment will be the last thing on your mind.

THE SONG YOU HEARD
SINGING IN THE LEAF
WHEN YOU WERE A CHILD
IS SINGING STILL.

-MARY OLIVER

Do we travel to other worlds a lot in the Afterlife?

There is no travel in the Afterlife. Anything you can think of you can manifest in the Afterlife. If you want to manifest another world to explore, you just create it in front of you. It is so beyond anything you could hope for, Rain! Think of the best thing you can imagine and multiply it times a million!

Do people have jobs in the Afterlife? What do we do all day?

There is no need for money in the Afterlife because you can manifest whatever you desire just by thinking it. Not many beings choose to spend their day working a job. There is no need for it. Who serves you dinner at restaurants? Usually clones. Or you can choose to cook for one another and serve one another. But you do this for love. So, there is no need to work a meaningless job and no need to work a job for money.

So, you have time for meaningful work in the Afterlife?

That is right. Each of us has something we are good at; something we are known for. We share our gifts with one another and contribute to the highest good of all that is. For example, Jazzabelle* is one of the best doggies in the Macroverse. She is so happy and so loving, that other dogs want to learn from her. So, she teaches others about the joy of service and the joy of being a dog. I am known for my singing ability. I teach others to improve their singing abilities. We each get to do what we love, as often as we like, for the betterment of all.

** Mom's 14 year old Golden Retriever who passed a few years before Mom*

Is there anything you do not like about the Afterlife?

That you, Jeremy, Laura, and my grandkids aren't here yet! Other than that, no, there is nothing I would wish to change about the Afterlife. It is SO wonderful and SO amazing, it is beyond description. Every single day on EARTH, you feel pain. Sometimes it is physical, sometimes emotional, sometimes spiritual, but always, always, painful. I do not miss that. Not one bit. Seriously, Rain, it is ALL good in the Afterlife. Do not rush through your life to get here. However, once you transition, you are going to feel a sense of INCREDIBLE relief.

Do people exercise and do yoga in the Afterlife?

Absolutely. But no one <u>must</u> exercise to look or feel a certain way. Anything you enjoy on Earth can be enjoyed in the Afterlife but usually in a much more amplified way. For example, you may choose to take a yoga class cliffside next to crystalline ocean waters with dolphins and whales breaching in the distance. You can pick any time of day. Maybe you love sunset. You decide to do yoga at sunset by the ocean. However, not just any ordinary sunset, the most extraordinarily gorgeous sunset you could ever imagine! Maybe you invite five of your favorite friends. You co-create the experience together. Perhaps you become mermaids and swim with the dolphins, or you become light dragons and fly through the air.

Do you get the idea? The fun never ends! It is the most magical existence you could ever imagine. It is heaven. This is what heaven means. You get to do absolutely anything you want at any time! It is constant play and creativity!

Is there entertainment in the Afterlife? Like TV and movies?

There is entertainment but it is always in person. There are no phones, tvs, or movie theaters. There is no need for travel or even things like holograms because you can manifest anything you want in any moment you want.

Is there shopping in the Afterlife?

There is no money or need for shopping in the Afterlife. Anyone can recreate the experience of it if they choose. However, shopping is something I would really indulge in if I were back in the game.

What about music?

Music in the Afterlife is IN-credible! It is WAY beyond anything you have ever experienced on Earth. It defies explanation. However, my advice is to enjoy music while you are on Earth. Earth-born music has a certain characteristic about it...a uniqueness. Music born from suffering sounds different than music born in the Afterlife. That difference is notable. Enjoy the uniqueness of Earth-born music.

Is there fashion in the Afterlife?

Not in a business sense. Fashion exists as an expression of pure creativity. Unlike Earth, fashion in the Afterlife is not limited by conditions. Fashion options are unlimited really. Therefore, Afterlife Fashion Shows are more like sharing creative ideas with one another. It is inspiring and fun!

What about skincare, makeup and hairstyles?

Thankfully, nothing is needed to prepare you for anything. You simply decide how you would like to look and you do. You can change anything about the way you look in an instant. There is no need for hair products and makeup, Rain. All commerce is unique to incarnation.

EVERY WALL IS A DOOR.

-RALPH WALDO EMERSON

Wow. We are going to have so much more free time in the Afterlife!

Well, you definitely do not have to spend any time getting ready! And there is no dissatisfaction in the way you look because you are able to express yourself however you intend. It is pretty cool when you think about it compared to Earth; no medicine, no nutrition, no working out, no sleeping, no stretching, absolutely nothing is needed to continue in your most optimum form!

That is a huge relief, Mom. Especially when I think about the hours and hours every day we spend eating, drinking, working out, stretching, getting ready, getting dressed. It is a full-time job! You must feel SO FREE!

I can tell you one thing for sure, Rain. The moment you pass over, you want to scream for joy! The overwhelming feeling of relief and gratitude is indescribable. It is a freedom unlike anything you have ever known.

What do you mean? How would you describe it?

It is beyond any words I could use to describe it. It is so incredible. It is a dream come true. You can create anything you want. You are a creator of worlds. You are a creator of universes. Every single being is capable of reaching their highest potential. Living at a higher frequency is simply a choice, like tuning a radio station.

So, do you live in a "Home" like we do here on Earth?

Yes, most everyone has a main "home" but it is not the same as on Earth because you do not require any sleep in the Afterlife. So, there is no requirement that you spend any time at home. Many souls explore extensively and don't spend very much time at home. Other souls prefer to stay around their own home so they can build and create.

Do people eat out at restaurants in the Afterlife?

Yes, we have some of the most exquisite restaurants to choose from! But every individual is allowed their own unique experience. Most people prefer to have a famous chef cook their meal somewhere stunningly gorgeous...on a yacht, an island, the top of a mountain.... Few people want to be contained inside a building.

Do you still digest food?

Only if you really want to, and not many people miss digesting food! Most enjoy the taste of eating and the feeling of being full, but have the feeling instantly go away the moment they are ready. Why go through digestion when your bodies no longer require it? Most of us just choose to feel absolutely incredible all of the time...the best we have ever felt!

That honestly sounds way more fun than eating food....

We still gather for meals and go through the enjoyment of eating, but we also get to feel the most amazing we have ever felt at the same time. You get both, Rain. And more.

What is the most popular food choice in the Afterlife?

Across the board, ice cream and chocolate are the most requested foods to eat in the Afterlife. Everyone seems to have their favorite meal from the EARTH game, something that reminds them of home on EARTH. Many who lived in America choose to eat pizza and drink soda.

Do individuals drink alcohol in the Afterlife?

You can do anything you like in the Afterlife. If you want to go through the experience of drinking alcohol and feeling dizzy like you used to on Earth, you can certainly do that. However, we "feel" a million times better than you have ever felt while drinking alcohol. So, the reality is I do not know anyone who drinks alcohol.

However, you can create a drink with any experience you would like to have. If you wanted to drink something you enjoyed on Earth, you just think of it and it manifests. The issue is that most of us can imagine a drink way better than Earth's alcohol. Imagine a "love potion" that covers you in waves of love. Or you drink something that makes you shine brighter and brighter with every sip. There are endless possibilities.

Gender & Parenthood in the Afterlife

Is there gender in the Afterlife?

Yes and no. We spend more time shapeshifting between forms than spending too much time in any one form. It is our form of play and creative expression. Gender is simply an expression one can choose to experience or not. It is not uncommon to shapeshift in between genders. The gender fluidity you are experiencing on Earth is taking you one step closer to your true eternal nature—genderless.

If two individuals are parent-child within the EARTH game, will they always be parent-child, even in the Afterlife?

Not necessarily, Rain, but they will always, always be Soul Family, connected beyond the confines of Space and Time and the lower vibrational Earth reality.

Do people have families in the Afterlife?

Yes, but families in the Afterlife are MUCH larger and more extended than on EARTH.

What about children? And childbirth?

It is much different on Earth than in the Afterlife. There is no pregnancy or painful childbirth in the Afterlife, unless you specifically choose to experience it. Lol.

Do you miss some of the hard work associated with Earth? Is it too easy for you now?

That is funny, Rainey. Lol! Not for one moment. It is like asking people who rode wagons across the US if they would miss riding wagons once they discover they can go by plane. The answer is no. You will never, ever want to revert to your lower vibrational experience of living. You may do it out of love for one another or compassion for all that is. But you will not return because things are too good in the Afterlife and you are bored.

The Best Things About the Afterlife

Tell me something you love about the Afterlife?

The fact that anything is possible is really exciting for me. This was emphasized for me by my Earth experience. I spent so much of my incarnation trapped in limited thinking. It is fun and exciting for me to exercise the power of my imagination. I feel like I spent my entire lifetime on Earth and barely used it! Once it *really* started to sink in that I could create absolutely **anything** I could imagine, I started to have **so much fun!** I forgot how creative I naturally am and what wonderful, unique things I can manifest. When you return Home, Rain, I will show you some of the things I have created just with my imagination.

I can't wait, Mom! Could you share five things you love about the Afterlife?

(1) There is music everywhere. Amazing, beautiful music.

(2) Anything you can imagine, you can instantly create.

(3) Good is everywhere, negativity is nowhere to be found.

(4) Physicality is only one of thousands, even millions, of senses.

(5) There is no death. You live for eternity. There is no aging.

Wow! It is going to be really difficult to finish out this Earth incarnation....

It will go by in the blink of an eye, Rain, so please do not rush it! Just know that you *already have* won the lottery. You have everything you could ever wish, hope for, or desire. You have just forgotten momentarily.

Know that when you return Home, it is going to be the BIGGEST, most amazing celebration you could ever imagine! You will be reunited with your Twin Flame and your true Soul Family. It will feel like a tidal wave of unconditional love is washing over you. You will feel so relieved when you understand that all the problems of Earth have already been resolved in the Afterlife. Overwhelming joy will come rushing over you when you wake up inside your dream home on the top of the mountain overlooking the ocean. Everything you could ever want or dream of is waiting for you when you return to us. Your home is perfect, clean, comfortable, overflowing with abundance, opulence…just waiting for you.

When I close my eyes Mom, I can see it!

Your home overlooks a perfectly clear crystalline ocean containing rainbow diamond-sparkling water! There are *always* dolphins, whales, and mer-people swimming and playing. But better than everything you see, the Afterlife is so amazing because you *feel* amazing *all* of the time!

There are no words to describe what a wonderful, beautiful contrast it is to the Earth experience. This is not to say that EARTH is bad, it is only that the Afterlife is SO MUCH BETTER. Compare an old school Atari video game to living on Earth in a body. A million times different, right? Well, the Afterlife is a million times different than EARTH.

CHAPTER 3

We are Always Tuned into Earth

Ok Mom, please tell us what the heck is going on here on Earth?

Earth is not what you think, Rain. It is an illusion! I swear! Everything you see is written in code. Earth is a simulation. It is a reproduction, like a virtual reality game. Everyone on Earth voluntarily chose to participate/incarnate into the game, including you. We refer to it as EARTH in all capital letters.

Wow! That is a lot to swallow. Could you explain it in more detail?

Sure, Rain. Essentially EARTH is a virtual playing field—a learning tool—where we seek to gain greater understanding of the implications of certain courses of action. For example, many worst-case scenario events play out on EARTH so that we may gain greater clarity surrounding the consequences of certain actions. We seek greater awareness through observation. We attempt to resolve all issues on EARTH without external intervention.

Why are we participating in it?

It is by choice. You are there to become alchemists in human form. The rules of the Earth game are being slowly revealed to you.

What the actual heck, Mom? An *illusion?* How are we supposed to digest that information?

I know it is a lot to grasp, honey. But it is the truth. You are participating in one of the most vivid, realistic, virtual reality "games" in existence. All your hard work and achievements **have** made a difference. Everything you have done within the game has been for an important, meaningful purpose. Every single life matters within EARTH.

A Simulation to Guide us All

Can you tell us a little bit more about this "game"?

EARTH is hands down the most popular "virtual reality game" in the Macroverse. I am hesitant to use the word "game" because I know you and every person reading these words are shouting back at me in this moment— *"This is not a game!! People are suffering, the planet is being pillaged, entire animal species are going extinct, our water and food supplies are corrupted, our loved ones are dying...."*

That is 100% how I feel, Mom!

Trust me, I hear you! I have a vivid memory of my time on EARTH. The pain of certain experiences still stings at times. So, instead of calling it a "game," we will refer to EARTH as an educational experience—a simulation. This simulation is important to preventing existence-wide suffering. As our best and brightest go into EARTH with the highest hopes, the Macroverse watches in rapt attention.

So, this is what you mean when you say that our loved ones in the Afterlife are always tuned in to EARTH?

That is exactly right, Rain! It is the most popular show in the Macroverse. It truly guides us all.

Hold on a second, Mom. You are trying to tell me that not only are we living in a simulation, but it is educational in nature?

That is right, Rain. It is not a game that people just "play" for fun. Entering into the EARTH simulation is not easy. It takes time to get selected. There is literally a gigantic waiting list to get inside of EARTH. Every soul in the Macroverse wants to play because the experience is known far and wide as the most challenging "game" ever. Also, many souls want to incarnate into the game because they know that what happens inside of EARTH has a huge impact on how decisions are made throughout the Macroverse.

So, you are saying EARTH is a guiding force for everyone in the Afterlife?

That is right, Rain. It is not a video game as you would think of one in your modern era. It is a near-exact simulation of a real time on Earth in its past history.

Resist much, obey little.

-Walt Whitman

Hold up. So, is the Afterlife the future? And I live in a pretend world that seems 100% realistic and is plagued by numerous problems of the past that have already been resolved?

Yes, exactly!

So, how far in the future is the Afterlife compared to present day Earth?

There is no time in the Afterlife but if we were to compare, it is as if we are over one million years more advanced than EARTH.

So, EARTH is reliving a time in ancient history?

We had to make the game realistic and believable. We also had to go back far enough when the Earth was still overrun with problems. We have tried various time periods in the EARTH game and feel the modern age you are currently living in is the best for our educational purposes.

What do you say to the people who are reading this chapter thinking, *WTF? A virtual reality game? You've got to be kidding me!*

I say this. Please do not feel that I am trying to convince you of something. I am not trying to make you believe in anything. I am simply sharing my perspective. I promised you I would tell the truth, Rain, no matter how shocking, and that is what I am doing.

Let us be very clear here. Rainey, it took you almost **five** years to digest this information before you were ready to write about it. So, I would say to any reader who is having an unexpected or intense reaction, extend compassion to yourself. You do not have to agree with me. You do not need to believe me. You do not even need to *read* this chapter! You can skip it entirely. It does not matter. It is here if you are interested and if not, just move on and let go of it, especially if the information upsets you.

I agree with you completely, Mom. If any concept ever upsets a reader or makes them feel uncomfortable in a negative way, I always encourage those readers to pick and choose what they read. Forcing readers to take every book and read it left to right in its entirety is very limiting and left-brained. A book should be felt. Intuition should guide the reader what to read.

Exactly. Your intuition will always lead you in the right direction. It is your own internal truth meter. There is an open-mindedness and a readiness to receive necessary to digest this information. I *know* this is a *lot* to handle. It would have been huge for me too. I do not know if I would have allowed myself to believe it. I imagine it would have taken me a long time to digest.

So, what do you say to people like you were when you were human?

I guess what I would tell people, Rain, is that it does not matter if you understand or believe **anything** related to the game, the simulation, and the illusion. This is simply information that I am sharing with you. Although you may be hearing about this concept for the first time, this is not new information by any stretch! There are a number of human beings right now within the game who are intimately familiar with what we are discussing. You may be hearing it for the first time, or you may be hearing about it in a new way, but this information regarding the nature of the game has been available to humanity throughout the existence of the game.

What are some of the signs or indications that humanity is in a simulation?

Look for glitches in the simulation. Things that are unexplained. Why is there weather modification? That was one of the most important aspects to the chemtrail question, Rain. Why was weather modification taking place *at all*? And why was it taking place across the globe over every single country and nation? Who has that much power? And who is paying for all of the planes and the millions of tons of chemicals being sprayed? Why is humanity not up in arms? Why is no one trying to stop it?

As you proceed down this line of thought, it becomes clear that no one within the game is controlling things. In fact, it is us, the makers of the game, outside of the simulation, controlling the game. But like I mentioned before, ***we are you.*** So, you really are the answer you seek.

Another indication of the simulation is the requirement for 7-8 hours of sleep every night....

More like 9-10 hours, Mom! Are you saying that we don't need sleep in the Afterlife?

That's right, Rain. Sleep is not necessary in the Afterlife. However, some people enjoy napping, or spending time sleeping in a comfortable bed. Some people like to sleep all the time. It really comes down to personal choice.

You mentioned that EARTH is a popular "game" with a rigorous selection process. Could you describe this process in greater detail?

Certainly. Most of the time, souls are selected for EARTH based on an Artificial Intelligence matching program of sorts. I will mention that we do not believe in "artificial" anything in the Afterlife. All is considered "alive" and all has meaning/purpose.

**Only those who will
risk going too far
can possibly find out
how far one can go.**

-T.S. Eliot

How does the matching program work?

It is a combination of need within EARTH for a certain frequency and a matching in resonance to the frequency of the soul matched for the assignment. Most importantly, there must be willingness and desire to incarnate into the game.

What happens once a soul is selected to participate in EARTH?

Every soul that is selected to incarnate into the game must pass through the Veil of Forgetting. Every soul that passes through the Veil is required to forget everything they know before birth.

Veil of Forgetting

What is this Veil of Forgetting?

Every soul who comes to EARTH is required to move through the Veil of Forgetting. Your soul moves energetically through a field of frequency which removes all conscious memory of who you are, where you are from, and what you are doing on the planet. This veil is a block to certain memories. This block is required to make the EARTH experience feasible. Every single soul who incarnates into the game must forget who they are and where they come from to truly experience life on EARTH.

What about you revealing the details of the simulation to me and anyone who reads this book?

This information has the potential to be quite disruptive, certainly. But in a good way. Like the internet or how electricity changed EARTH. Yes, it will be enormously disruptive for the great masses of humanity to know they are living within a simulation. However, the time for this information to come forward is now.

How does knowing this ultimately help humanity?

To begin with, I am not sharing this information with you for that purpose. I am sharing this information with you because it is the truth. It will help others regain their perspective and not feel so lost on EARTH. With this greater perspective, it is much easier to make it through a lifetime within the game. You know that you will soon be back in paradise and that this is only a brief experience you are having. I feel this will come as a big relief for a lot of people.

I want to be very clear, Rain. I *know* this is a lot to process. It is not something humanity must integrate. It could take years, decades, millennia even, for this information to be widely known and processed by the masses of humanity. The reason we are writing this book together is to share the truth with those individuals who are ready to hear this perspective.

I can understand how some people many choose to live in ignorance, sort of like the guy eating the steak in *The Matrix.* I can also understand how some individuals may not be vibrationally ready for this information. But not me! This information helps SO much! It helps me continue another day. It gives perspective and meaning but also clarity as to why I was feeling such an internal tension of inconsistencies while incarnated on EARTH.

That is the reason, Rain. The information is now available for anyone who wants it. The answer is here for anyone who is curious.

The ecstasy is so short
but the forgetting so long.

-Walt Whitman

Has the EARTH simulation always felt like this one?

Great question! No. There have been eight versions of EARTH. You are currently participating in the 7th Edition of the EARTH game and ascending as a species to the 8th Version of the game. These are details we can dive into later.

What is outside of the simulation?

What is outside of the simulation is the Afterlife, or "real life" as we call it. Despite how real EARTH may seem to you while you are in it, even if you were to explore to the edges of the Macroverse while incarnated, it would still only be a replica of the real thing. In fact, much of the magic from real life cannot be recreated within the game. You will understand the amazingness of what I am telling you once you transition and return Home. To answer the question, **everything** is outside of the simulation. Outside of the simulation is where real life exists.

Was there a time before the simulation? Before the game?

Certainly, yes. Of course, there is no time. There are only moments to experience. Our experience in the Afterlife before the simulation was not quite as fulfilling, inspiring or complete as it has been since the creation of EARTH. Therefore, we have replaced an incomplete memory with the reality of a more complete experience. There may come a time *after* the simulation, but we have not reached that point yet. We see the EARTH experience in all directions and moments surrounding us.

Why don't we spend some time talking about *why?* Why would someone in the Afterlife want to voluntarily incarnate into this game of EARTH?

Great question, Rain. Let's jump into that question in the next chapter.

Chapter 4

You are Revered by All

Ok Mom, why would we want to leave the Afterlife to participate in the suffering of Earth?

You came to EARTH because you wanted to help. You are high vibrational beings of light and love. You heard the call for assistance, and you answered it. You cannot imagine how revered you are for your sacrifice. Everyone knows what a challenge it is to incarnate. Upon transitioning to the other side, many souls report that this was their most difficult incarnation.

I can confirm that, Mom! Please tell me it will all be worth it....

It will all be worth it, Rain! In the Afterlife, many souls who lived EARTH lives are easily recognizable because everybody has been tuning in to watch.

Are you saying we are like rockstars? Lol!

That is right! In addition to being easily recognizable, the level you reach in the EARTH game expresses itself in the form of auric colors you "wear" for all of eternity. Others will be able to see a color frequency representing an Earth incarnation. They will be in awe of you and will ask you to share stories. It may not be fun while you are in there, Rain, but I promise it pays off in the Afterlife!

It will be a lot more fun when I am looking back on this life and telling stories. Right now, I am in the thick of human emotion.

I know it can be hard, Rain. Just remember, you came to EARTH because you believed that your contribution would be hugely significant and beneficial. You knew you *had* to incarnate. You are doing it for a bigger purpose, Rain.

As long as I know it is helping humanity, then I suppose it is worth it.

Remember Rainey, those of you who were able to maintain a high frequency in the midst of Version 7, will always be revered for your contribution. You are revered by all.

What exactly is it about the EARTH experience that is so important to the Afterlife?

EARTH is the location for all less-than-ideal scenarios to be played out so that we may learn from the consequences. This means learning the result without actually implementing the lower vibrational experience. Thus, we avoid a TON of unnecessary pain and suffering by having possibilities play out on EARTH first.

Mom, are humans on EARTH viewed as not real because we are inside of a game? Is it like you really do not feel that we are suffering because we chose to participate in the first place?

I know that is something that has always bothered you – the perception that the pain and suffering experienced inside the game of EARTH is not perceived as "real" by those of us in the Afterlife. But what you should know, Rain, is that not only are your experiences and feelings valued, but every single decision you make while on EARTH is something all of us can learn from. Never, ever discount the significance of your contribution to existence!

If we are so important then why can't you intervene to help us?

We cannot intervene, *at all*. It is one of the strict rules of EARTH. We jump into that more in the next chapter.

Can you give me the *Cliff Notes* version?

Ok fine. Here you go. We cannot have those in the Afterlife who remember everything interfering with a game that requires an absolute forgetting of every single player. It would affect the outcome of the game and remove the essential component of learning that is necessary for real world. Then all your "suffering" would be for nothing!

I get it...it makes sense...but it really sucks so much not having help while inside the game.

Remember that while you will not have external intervention on your behalf, you are entitled to have the assistance of voluntary Guardian Angels (like I am to you). We can help you with the little things (making the green light, getting the interview, winning the contract) but we may not influence things on a bigger scale. It is a very strict rule of the game.

Thank you, Mom, for being my Guardian Angel!

You are most welcome, Rain.

How Earth is Perceived from the Afterlife

What do beings in the Afterlife think about EARTH?

It is Macroversally well-known that the EARTH game is very, very challenging. It is known by all to easily be the most difficult game ever designed. It is challenging to even get selected to participate in the EARTH game. The vast majority of EARTH incarnates fail miserably on their missions. There is no judgment in this because successfully remembering anything about the Afterlife while in the game, is extremely rare and nearly impossible.

What percentage of EARTH incarnates are able to remember their soul mission/purpose while they are on EARTH?

Only three percent, Rain! Can you believe it?! Only 3 %! This is why almost everyone chooses to reincarnate and do better the next time.

TO LIVE IS SO STARTLING, IT LEAVES LITTLE TIME FOR ANYTHING ELSE.

-EMILY DICKINSON

Are a lot of beings in the Afterlife paying attention to what is happening on EARTH?

Pretty much every, single living being in the Afterlife is tuned into EARTH all day, every day. Like I said, it is by far the most popular game in the Macroverse. Just like humans watch reality TV shows, we tune in to watch our favorite players in the game facing the daily challenges of being human. It is very difficult for people watching to understand why anyone would voluntarily enter this game. It is so challenging, so harsh, so unfair, so brutal...but most importantly, so vastly different from real life. Real life in the Afterlife, I mean!

Do you think about times on EARTH? Do you spend much time in memory?

Having the perspective that includes the reason behind everything really allows us to not cling too tightly to what is happening on EARTH. There is way too much for us to do to be trapped in memories. We know that ultimately, it is only a game, an experience. We also know that we can learn from absolutely everything that happens within the game. Does this not relieve you from carrying the burden related to this?

Completely, yes, Mom!! I need to also remember to call on you for help.

Yes, that is right. I am here whenever you need me, just ask. Remember, Guardian Angels are always tuned into loved ones. We are always, *always* at your side. We can assist any time you ask. It is important to remember to ask.

What do you say to people who have lived torturous lives of abuse and mental enslavement on EARTH?

You are not alone. You knew what you would go through before incarnating and you willingly volunteered to face it within this lifetime. Try not to fall into self-pity or sadness. Allow yourself to see the larger picture and the true reason you decided to incarnate in the first place. Once you begin to remember the truth of who you are, you will know within the depths of your soul that your contribution was integral in preventing suffering within the Afterlife. Once you remember the true warriors and leaders you are deep inside, you will no longer feel sorry for yourselves. You will remember your spiritual, preincarnation contracts and let everything else go.

What about those people who say that Utopia cannot exist because we would just get too bored of being "good" all the time?

Those people invented the EARTH game! They believed deep within their souls that evil, darkness, and contrast must exist for good to flourish. However, this theory has already been played out in the Afterlife and the theory has been disproven. Anyone you ask in the Afterlife would say yes, Utopia exists and yes, Heaven is real. You will, however, find differing opinions on whether the negativity of EARTH is important to the evolution and positive growth of all that is.

So, should we think about this life as a work assignment or a business trip?

That is funny, Rain. Yes, you certainly could! However, you will have a much more fun, fulfilling life if you approach it like an adventure as opposed to a work assignment.

It will be over before you know it. Remember that your soul, your authentic self, never leaves Eternity. This is the truth of oneness. You are an integral piece of all that is...of source; the source of love itself. That is who you are always.

But I definitely feel like I am on Earth and not in Eternity!

You could have millions of incarnations happening all at once. Only you decide how much of your soul inhabits the body and how much stays behind to keep you grounded in the truth of who you are. Earth is just a temporary experience. Enjoy it. Relish it. Do not spend one second in a bad mood. You are an eternal being. Always. This can never be changed. So play, enjoy, but do not despair. Do not resist life. It is a privilege and will be over before you know it.

I am glad there is an educational benefit to all of our suffering but seriously, is it really worth it? Do you remember how difficult it was to be a human?

Oh, I remember all right, Rain. It is almost torture. At least you know that it is all worth it in the end.

I am just saying that I hope this game is extremely educational given how much suffering we are having to endure within it. Some days it is so hard!

I know, Rain. That is why I am saying to suck it up and get through it because the entire Macroverse is depending on you.

No pressure then?

That is funny, Rain!

Mom, can you summarize this chapter?

Incarnating into the game of EARTH is looked upon highly by All That Is. Becoming an EARTH incarnate is a competitive process. Selection can take eons. It is most important to live your best life. Make the most of your incarnation. Yes, you have suffered great losses. However, everything you do is honored and revered at the highest levels. We understand how challenging an EARTH incarnation is and we have great empathy for those of you in the game.

Chapter 5

We Wish We Could Help You More

OK Mom, why can't you directly intervene on Earth?

Given the nature of EARTH, those of us in the Afterlife collectively agree that intervention into the EARTH game would have a disastrous outcome on the information we receive from the game. Our intervention could mean that all the suffering and sacrifice of previous incarnates would be for nothing. Therefore, intervention of any sort has been strictly forbidden.

You know this is a HUGE issue for me, Mom. I'm sorry, please, slow down and help me understand. This sounds like such BS!

The entire purpose of EARTH to begin with was to play out scenarios to discover outcomes underneath the strict conditions of the game. Each and every player knows that sacrifices made inside the game may prevent problems from happening outside of the game, in the Afterlife. We make sacrifices within the game to maintain the vibrational purity of the Afterlife.

The Simulation Must Stay Pure

I get all of that, yes. But what is the point of allowing the suffering to continue after the lesson has been learned?

We are always waiting to see if humanity can pull through. If so, that changes the results quite dramatically. It affects the way we address things in the Afterlife. The EARTH game must be <u>**really real**</u> in order for us to learn from it. We don't seem to learn as much from simple games. It is only in the very real illusory reality of the EARTH game that beings reveal how they would *really* act when times get tough. It is a constant ocean of learning for us.

It just seems like an excuse. How could more good come from something negative? Doesn't the greatest amplification of good come from more good?

The results of the EARTH game confirm that more good can come from both the same and the opposite. There is need for some contrast, for the highest good of all that is to really reach the highest frequency. This is why the EARTH game continues and is so popular. In fact, the popular idea on Earth that good only comes from more good, is actually not accurate. You will discover this as humanity evolves. This is why the experiment continues. We are learning just as much from inside of the experiment as we are learning from outside the experiment. We are able to avoid so much suffering by watching scenarios play out on EARTH. We observe the consequences and know not to make the same mistakes. Do you understand now? We 100% cannot intervene or we would lose all of the gains made through EARTH incarnation.

Star Children

Does anyone transition from an Earth incarnation into the Afterlife and beg you to intervene?

Not a lot of people do this, but the ones who do are very, very adamant that humanity needs assistance. The cries for help were heard and the response was to send in the star children to the EARTH game.

Who are the star children, Mom?

Star children are higher vibrational incarnates ("old souls") imprinted with the soul purpose of assisting those in the game with reaching peace. The star children are highly sensitive, highly evolved, and highly compassionate souls who incarnate into suitable homes on EARTH.

Why were the star children selected to incarnate?

The key part of our very strict nonintervention policy is that the only intervention that is allowed is for another to incarnate into the game. The only real assistance you may receive is from one another. It is no secret to those of us in the Afterlife as to how difficult the game of EARTH is, overall. Only the bravest and most noble souls are even *able* to incarnate in the first place. However, even these gorgeous souls get lost. Even the best lose their way on EARTH. It is the way of the game.

If suffering brings wisdom,
I would wish that I
were less wise.

-William Butler Yeats

So, the reality is a lot of souls incarnate with big plans and then lose their way in the game?

Big plans, yes. However, not a lot of souls volunteer to go into the game with the soul purpose of saving humanity. Most keep their expectations low, knowing they will be lucky to get out alive, or at least with their soul still intact. It is an extremely dangerous mission and one that is not taken lightly.

Are you saying that some have experienced permanent soul damage?

There are those that report permanent damage, like PTSD on their souls, from being inside the game. The level of difficulty was just far too much for most. From inside the game, it is described as a tidal wave of negativity and toxicity washing over incarnates daily. The conditions in Version 7 of the game have reached a point of becoming almost unbearable.

Suicides in the Game

What do you mean unbearable?

Most incarnates reported back that the game was too difficult, the conditions were too awful, and life inside was simply too bitter to swallow. The majority of incarnates, even our best and brightest, were heavily involved in escapist activities such as gambling, drugs, and alcohol. However, what concerned us most were the exponential increase in mental disorders and suicides.

Have there been a lot of suicides?

Rain, what you must realize is that never before, in six previous versions of the game—six epochs—has any soul left the game through suicide. The natural tendency towards survival kept everyone inside of the game. It was not until this current version of the game (Version 7) that we experienced a massive increase in souls praying, crying, and begging for help. We still refused to intervene in any direct manner. This has resulted in a massive number of suicides within the game.

Really? Why have we not heard about it?

It is definitely something we would like to keep quiet. We need participation in the simulation for it to hold the most educational value. We would not want incarnates looking to suicide as an easy exit.

Well, is it? An easy exit?

I most certainly do not want to endorse suicide in any form or fashion. Regardless of what happens when you die, the effects left behind are like a bomb exploding. Suicide is always selfish and is always immediately regretted after passing over.

What happens to someone who commits suicide when they die?

The same thing happens to them as happens to everyone else. It is no different. They go through the exact same transition process including a Life Review, although a Council is always present for suicides.

So, there is no judgment, no punishment?

That is exactly right. The only judgment and punishment is self-inflicted when the individual sees the damaging legacy their suicide left behind. It is always, always the better choice to live out your life as you had planned and contracted prior to incarnation. You will regret ending it early. I promise. Plus, it goes by in the blink of an eye!

Fear of regret is not what holds me back, Mom. It is fear that I will have to re-enter the EARTH game and start all over!

Your fear is not unfounded. Almost every single soul who passes over from suicide immediately reincarnates to do it over, and better, next time. It is a personal choice, yes, but one that is unavoidable with suicide.

Mom, you know as well as I do that there is a zero percent chance I am coming back to do this again so suicide is not a viable option for me.

That truth is what keeps the masses of souls from exiting through suicide. However, we did hear the complaints and prayers of a great number of incarnates. These pleas fueled the fire for the creation of Version 8, which is a much more harmonious and pleasant version than you are currently experiencing.

Just how prevalent is suicide within Version 7?

A massive number of new incarnates were opting to choose suicide over a life of mental enslavement. Of those who were more seasoned at the game, the percentage was lower. The problem was highly disturbing to us in the Afterlife. We had created a game so torturous and awful that souls who had waited *eons* to incarnate were choosing to leave voluntarily and unnaturally. This was not something we wanted. This was not something we intended. We learned a great deal about ourselves because of this information. We are so deeply grateful to all the incarnates who suffered torturous lives on EARTH before ultimately giving up because the conditions were so oppressive. We felt, collectively, that we had crossed a line of sorts.

What do you mean?

EARTH had become our way of exploring the edges of possibility for all of existence. We were becoming more experienced with living on the edge, so to speak. Our future as eternal souls seemed to depend on it. We have learned to dance upon this edge, but not to cross over. Crossing over to where the game is more harmful than helpful is a place we do not ever want to land. Through direct experience we have learned that we do not want to cross that line, for learning or other purposes. The karmic repercussions are too great.

Version 8 is the Intervention

So, what did you do about this increase in suicide?

There is a Macroversal law that states that if 10% (or more) of humanity requests assistance through prayer or meditation from within the game, a new version of the game must be designed and all participants given the option to upgrade to the new version. This percentage had never been reached in the history of EARTH. Not until the 1987 – 2023 window.

So, you are saying that the creation of Version 8 was a response to global prayer?

Yes, as soon as this parameter was met, Version 8 went under construction. To protect those who have requested help, a quarantine was placed around EARTH so that no further abuse of power will take place. Once this critical point was reached, many high vibrational souls entered the game to become way showers of the higher version. This is what many call ascension.

Are you saying that ascension is not something woo? It just means upgrading to a newer version of EARTH?

Exactly. It means moving from version 7 to version 8 of EARTH.

Wow. This chapter has been a trip. Can you touch on the high points for us?

Those of us in the Afterlife cannot intervene with anything on EARTH. It is a strict rule that cannot be broken. We help you every chance we get. We wish we could help you more. We hate to see you suffer. It breaks our hearts when anyone leaves the game through suicide. Especially since we know how long that soul waited to incarnate. Every single one of you. Me included. It is never the right option, no matter how bad your incarnation seems.

The high incidence of suicide in version 7 along with the minimum percentage being reached when it came to prayers and requests for intervention, caused us to build version 8. Version 8 is all about harmony, peace, love, and joy. We created Version 8 because we love you. We created Version 8 because we are the makers of the game. We created Version 8 because we are also the incarnates into the game. We created Version 8 because we are you.

It always seems impossible until it is done.

Nelson Mandela

Chapter 6

Relationships are All that Matter

Positive relationships, moments of kindness, unconditional giving. My mom says these are the ONLY things you will look back on and say mattered. That's it. Everything else is a waste of breath. As my favorite poet, William Butler Yeats, said in *Vacillation*,

> *Begin the preparation for your death*
> *And from the fortieth winter by that thought*
> *Test every work of intellect or faith,*
> *And everything that your own hands have wrought*
> *And call those works extravagance of breath*
> *That are not suited for such men as come*
> *proud, open-eyed and laughing to the tomb.*

Nothing. Else. Matters. *Nothing.*

My mom's advice? Drop all conflict. End all division. Now

End Conflict Wisely

What are the best ways to end conflict?

It starts with creating more harmonious relationships. Notice the things you have in common with one another. Forget about the differences. Look for more ways to have fun with one another. Have more parties. Worry less. Spend more time in joy.

Why is it so important for us to end all conflict now?

All conflict on EARTH is a complete waste of energy. Not only does it take you away from your path, but it also drains you. The exact moment you cross over, you are hit with a wave of unconditional love and peace that exists in sharp contrast to any conflict you experienced on EARTH. It is not that you feel regret for all conflict experienced during incarnation, it is more that you feel regret for not staying at the highest vibration possible throughout your life.

Why will we regret not staying at our highest vibration?

The more conflict you have in your Earthly life, the more likely you will return through another incarnation to correct the soul level experience. Reincarnation into EARTH is how souls deal with this feeling of regret.

But isn't this conflict ultimately a good thing? Aren't we learning from it?

We seem to learn the most from how we handle challenging situations, tapping into human determination and will to overcome them. How does humanity create good out of the worst? How does one transmute evil into good? Overcoming conflict, transmuting discord, being energetic alchemists, and transforming friction into something better are things we work on through the EARTH simulation.

What about conflict caused by people who have treated us wrongly?

Turn the other cheek, but do not allow yourself to get slapped again. Step away from conflict. Transformation does not require you to be knee deep in negativity. Move away from it. There is nothing to be gained by martyrdom. You do not have to transform the source of negativity (the person), only the energy itself.

So, your advice is to turn the other cheek when someone wrongs us?

Yes, turn the other cheek, step away from conflict, focus on something else, and LET. IT. GO.

But what if someone treats us *really* badly? Like horribly wrong?

The very best thing you can do is to let it go and begin thinking of the things you *do* want in life. I am not saying to stay in an abusive relationship or to continue allowing someone to treat you badly. You *must* separate. Begin attracting better things into your life. Do not allow yourself to spend one millisecond in negativity.

Your task is not to seek love,
but merely to seek and find all
barriers within yourself that
you have built against it.

-Rumi

Do you have any other advice for dealing with negativity caused by someone who has wronged us?

Divert your attention to something else. Do not give any attention to people who have wronged you. Truly the reason for the conflict does not matter. Do not give any thought to *Why?* It makes no difference who is wrong and who is right. It does not matter if one side is completely wrong and the other side, completely right. All that matters is that you drop it, immediately. As quickly as possible. I *promise* you will wish you had not spent one second in conflict when you look back at your actions in a Life Review.

What was it about your Life Review that made you feel so strongly about this?

I was so disappointed in myself, Rain. I could not believe how much of my life I spent on catty, insignificant things. I was mortified by how much of my life I spent in gossip. Every single negative word you speak or low vibrational thought you think has an impact on your life experience. Rainey, I wasted SO much of my life in negative thought! I encourage no one to make the same mistakes I made!

Mom, are you saying you wanted to immediately reincarnate to do it better next time?

That is right, Rain. There was no question in my mind about reincarnating again after observing my Life Review.

Is that how most people feel?

Ninety-seven percent of incarnates choose to reincarnate again. A mere three percent of incarnates choose to leave the game.

That is so surprising to me, Mom. Escape is literally all I can think about.

I know because your thoughts are public.

What do you mean, Mom, my thoughts are public?

Before you incarnated into the game of EARTH, you agreed to terms for your incarnation. You were fine with your thoughts being public for those of us in the Afterlife who are tuning in to EARTH.

Why?

Because you had confidence in the purity of your thoughts. You knew that if you could have a bad thought, anyone could. So, from an educational perspective, public observation would teach us more. It is why you came here after all.

I am okay with that. I don't have any thoughts I am trying to hide. I look forward to my Life Review! Bring it, baby!

Well, that was certainly the attitude you had when you signed up for this incarnation!

And look it where it got me, lol!

Well, the truth is you really cannot complain about your incarnation because you 100% knew what you were getting into.

I know that now, but don't forget that I have spent my entire life trying to figure out what was going on here! Now that I know, I can breathe a sigh of relief.

It is <u>such</u> a relief to share this information with you! I know how important these answers are to your life.

Relationships in the Afterlife

What are relationships like in the Afterlife?

What an amazing question, Rain. Relationships are so wonderful, so fulfilling, so incredible beyond description...I do not even know where to begin! Every single relationship is expressed beautifully, in its own unique way. Unconditional love and affection are freely given and received. Intimacy is not shared as freely. Intimacy is reserved for close soul family members, best friends, and partners.

Do we have sex in the Afterlife?

Yes, but it is always consensual. There is no sexual harm or abuse in the Afterlife so the intimate experience of physical sex is still participated in by willing souls. It is not something many do without consciousness or intimacy. Therefore, most intimacy, most sex, most super close relationships, are reserved for one or a few, depending on one's preference.

Now that your perspective has widened, how common are bad relationships on EARTH?

Rainey, you would be so shocked and horrified if you knew how many people—women in particular—are currently in an abusive relationship. It is a serious problem on EARTH. For the most part, women have been unable to pull themselves out and thrive on their own. This is beginning to slowly change. In truth, EARTH is almost impossible to go through alone. Everyone would like a partner. Unfortunately, partnerships within the game have such a low chance of succeeding. It is pretty much impossible for two people in a relationship to both hold consistently high vibrations. The reality is that one person drops and the relationship does not succeed.

Do you think these abusive relationships are in part caused by the false search for a twin flame on EARTH?

I do. To be clear, Twin Flame relationships are 100% real in the Afterlife. They just are not real on EARTH. To search for one's Twin Flame while in the EARTH game is to take you off of the path you chose to walk before you incarnated.

Twin Flames

Wait, why? Tell me more about Twin Flames. Does everyone have one?

Every single individual soul has a twin flame soul they are connected to at a very high frequency. The possibility for Twin Flame Love exists for every single individual. That being said, one's ability to access higher frequencies depends on that soul's personal path of evolution. So, the real question is not, *Does everyone have a Twin Flame?* But instead, *How many souls are able to access their Twin Flame relationship?*

The answer to that question is not many because *both* souls must have reached the higher frequencies to merge as one in the ultimate Twin Flame relationship. To experience Twin Flame love is one of the greatest experiences any soul can reach.

Ok then, what about Love? What is Love like in the Afterlife?

Every single individual has access to the greatest Love they have ever known in the highest form they can imagine. So, for some, Love means a constantly changing partner or a group of many partners...but for most in the Afterlife, we choose to have one partner, a Twin Flame if available. The Twin Flame relationship is considered the highest frequency Love relationship available. On Earth, often Twin Flames incarnate as parent-child, instead of adult partners, because the relationship maintains greater purity. The majority of Twin Flames do NOT incarnate together as romantic partners on EARTH.

What percentage of incarnates at this time are actual Twin Flames who have reunited into a relationship?

Ninety-nine percent of all incarnates have twin flames on the other side. This means they did NOT incarnate together into this life. I think once people realize that this is true, they will not spend so much of their life seeking something that they, frankly, will not find while on EARTH.

Why do most Twin Flames choose not to incarnate together?

Most Twin Flames know better than to incarnate at all. Instead, most attempt to help as Guardian Angels from the other side instead. The ones who cannot stay apart, came into EARTH as each other's pets or children. The few who do attempt to come as lovers end up going down in burning flames, to use a double entendre. It does not end well. Anything with that high of a vibration seems to crumble underneath the heavy, low vibrational frequencies of Version 7 of the EARTH game. There has not been a successful Twin Flame incarnation relationship yet.

Are there people out there putting up with an abusive relationship because they believe this person is their twin flame?

Yes, that is the tragedy in the false twin flame search. Most likely, their twin flame is not incarnated on EARTH. Even if they were, I can promise you would not want to experience such a beautiful relationship crushed by the weight of Earthly conditions.

So, are you saying that it is better to find a partner to get through the game with instead of searching for one's twin flame?

A million percent, yes, Rainey! Once people realize this, they will not put up with as much abuse from partners. They will also set more realistic expectations for their partners. Just look for someone who can partner with you through good times and bad. Release the crushing weight of expectations. Relationships on EARTH survive best when they are just allowed to *be*.

What advice would you give to people out there looking for their twin flame here on Earth?

First, I would send them love because seeking your twin flame is such a beautiful quest. Next, I would tell them that their energy is much better spent in other directions. The possibility of actually finding your twin flame on Earth is very, very small...almost zero. That fact aside, really take a moment to consider what being on Earth does to a relationship. Very few relationships on Earth ever thrive. There is deep degree of personal disappointment that comes from subjecting a twin flame relationship to Earth conditions. I do not recommend it.

So, are you saying that the search for one's twin flame on Earth is a waste of time?

Yes, completely. You are much better off focusing on other things that are possible to achieve while incarnated. Love is perfect in the Afterlife. You are all soon returning to perfect love. Do not seek perfect love within the imperfection of the Earth experience.

What would you focus on if you were us?

Instead of focusing on one relationship, I would focus on sharing love and light with a wider audience. I would try and disrupt the incarnation experience by remembering things I forgot before coming to Earth. Your purpose is to take thought to where it has never been before. You are on the leading edge of possibility. Know that. Play there. Do not get caught in the distractions of the Earth incarnation. Stay focused on why you incarnated in the first place.

So, are you basically saying if you were reincarnated again, you would not work a normal job?

That is absolutely what I am saying! I would do what I loved the most, every single day. I would sing for a living. I would sing for fun. I would sing just because I enjoyed it. I would sing just because. I would not do anything I did not thoroughly enjoy.

How would you pay bills? What about taxes?

I would outsource everything I did not enjoy doing myself. My singing would bring me great money because of how much I love singing. So, my passion would be my job. I recommend that everyone do what they love absolutely every day, even if they cannot make a living at it. It is absolutely essential for one's individual health, wellbeing, and longevity.

To be clear, I am not saying to stop participating in the illusion. I am just saying to not subject yourself to unnecessary suffering. I would encourage all humans to release the belief that they must suffer to achieve. That is one of the first beliefs every single human on EARTH must let go of to ascend to Version 8.

Choose the Higher Path

What advice would you give to someone reading this who wants to have a pleasant Life Review?

Devote your life to service to others. End all conflict. Any time you want to react, choose love instead. Always, always, always, choose the higher path. You will NOT regret it!

Are you 100% sure that what you are experiencing as the Afterlife is not also part of the simulation?

Great question, Rain! Yes, we are 100% sure. We exist at the vibration of Truth so there really is no question about it. The Afterlife, "real life," exists outside of the simulation. Only those incarnated into the game of EARTH are inside of the simulation. This can include off-planet beings, not necessarily just humans. Any soul incarnated into the EARTH game is part of the simulation. Only souls who are inside of the game can be tricked. There is no hiding of truth in the Afterlife. All is revealed.

Those of us outside of the simulation are able to observe any point within the simulation as it is happening, in real time, or moment to moment.

Do you guys watch our private moments?

No. Prior to your incarnation, you signed a soul-level agreement where you stated what you were and were not available for regarding observation. Most people choose to have private time in the bathroom or bedroom as off-limits. Others do not like to be watched while eating, or meditating. Therefore, those would be off limits to observation. There are other people who do not care at all. There are some who restrict who may or may not observe them.

Can we control our audience in any one moment?

Yes, absolutely. You can choose to allow or disallow observation at any moment. Your choice in any one moment will override any existing agreements put into place prior to incarnation. Ultimately, the higher frequency your choice, the better your reality

What are the best ways to end conflict?

It starts with creating more harmonious relationships. Notice the things you have in common with one another. Forget about the differences. Look for more ways to have fun with one another. Have more parties. Worry less. Spend more time in joy.

Mom, could you summarize the most important points in this chapter?

End all conflict. Stay in your highest vibration. Relationships are the only thing that matters. Do not spend this incarnation searching for your twin flame. That is not why you came to EARTH. Do what you love. Follow your heart. Find harmony with others.

The big question is whether you are going to be able to say a hearty yes to your adventure.

Joseph Campbell

CHAPTER 7

Laughter is More Important than Oxygen

What is the most important thing that we must know above all else?

Above all else, the most important thing you must do, absolutely every single day, is to LAUGH. Laughter is the most important thing you can do for your health and wellbeing. The more you laugh, the longer you live. On Earth, laughter is considered optional. In reality, laughter is more important than oxygen.

So, what do you recommend we laugh at?

Well, to start with, consider your incarnation. Lol.

Good one, Mom!

Laugh at whatever you find funny. Watch funny movies. Look at baby animals on social media. Do whatever makes you laugh. Laugh at yourself. The human incarnation is actually quite hilarious once you allow yourself to lighten up about it.

How is laughing good for us?

Laughing is not only good for the soul, but also for the physical body. After laughing, you will notice a lightness in your heart chakra. This is a vibrational lifting that stays with you for several hours following a great laugh. Try to laugh really, really, well at least once a day. Make it a goal to laugh until you pee your pants!

I remember you and your sister Laura laughing that hard!

That is right, Rain! I love my sister Laura so much. We always spent so much of our time together laughing so hard we cried. That laughing actually extended my life by several years. And Laura's. It was one of the things in life I am really proud of—I was good at laughing and I did it often.

You were the BEST!

Laughter is an extremely important tool in transforming ill health to good health. Finding humor brings a lightness to your chakras that actually clears the chakras of low vibrational energy. So, laugh daily, ideally laugh often many times each day for optimal health.

Sometimes it is hard for me to find any movies or shows that I actually find funny.

One of the realities of being inside of the illusion is that so much of the widely-accepted humor is based upon lower vibrational energies. The challenge of being a human is finding things that make you laugh that are of a higher vibration. For example, animals are a wonderful way to get a laugh. So are children. Watch funny short videos of animals and children. Their vibration is pure and innocent. So, laughing at animals and children is typically a light, higher vibration.

So, it is not good to laugh at other people?

There are better ways to raise your vibration. It is better to laugh at innocence than to make fun of others. Try your best to be kind and compassionate with every single human being you encounter.

What about animals? What about bugs?

Always, always choose to act with compassion, with animals and with bugs. Choose to save them when possible. Put them outside if you find bugs in your house. Be kind and compassionate to all animals you encounter. They are often loved ones who simply did not want to come in as a human. The wait list is much shorter for animals, given the current EARTH conditions for animals. Also, EARTH lives for animals are much shorter and easier to endure.

What do you laugh at in the Afterlife?

We laugh ALL the time in the Afterlife! It is one of the best things about existence—humor. We make each other laugh a lot. We can transform into animals and do funny things. It is super easy to laugh in the Afterlife. Laughter is a regular, moment-by-moment experience. In fact, when we observe the EARTH game, the first thing that seems shocking to us is how unhappy everyone seems. We feel there is a serious lack of laughter within the game. However, coming from my recent incarnation, I would say that is difficult to stay at a high vibration. Feeling really, truly happy is not something incarnates experience on EARTH.

That is the understatement of the millennia! What tangible advice can you give us to implement into our daily lives?

One piece of advice I would share with you would be to **spend more time in joy**! There are many reasons for this suggestion including raising your vibration and improving your subconscious or unconscious law of attraction ability by bypassing the mind and feeding the soul.

Why is being in joy so important?

Laughter and being in joy go hand in hand. They both have a similar frequency. Do your best to hold the high frequencies of laughter and joy and you will notice everything in your life changing for the better. You will feel better. You will hurt less. Life will flow more easily. You will experience better health.

How can we bring more joy into our lives daily?

My advice is wake up, focus on your breathing for a moment, even before opening your eyes. Pay attention to the coolness of the air coming in through your nose, the moment of heating the air in the back of your throat, and then slowly releasing the air through your nostrils, almost with an undercurrent of humming. The sooner in the day that you can begin to actively improve your vibration, the better.

So, start humming even before opening our eyes?

Yes! If you can, begin singing your favorite song as early in the day as possible. Turn up the music and sing and dance. Play with animals. Go outside. Receive information through sunlight. Be near the ocean. Submerge your feet into salt water. Laugh. Find joy. Watch the dolphins. Breathe in the ocean air. Think of all of the things you are grateful for and make a mental list. Visualize what you would like to manifest in your life. Do not spend any time focusing on what you do not want. Only focus on what you DO want.

It's All About Frequency

Why is singing out loud so important?

Singing out loud is a natural antidepressant! It is better than any medicine you could take. So, sing out loud as often as you possibly can! It does not matter if you have a good voice or an unpleasant voice. What matters is how you **feel** when you sing the song. How you feel inside is the most important thing you can do to enhance the effects of your singing. Feeling amazing while singing is like feeling amazing while manifesting. It is the perfect combination.

Let us pretend for a moment that you are back on Earth, but with full memory of the Afterlife, how would you live out 24 hours on Earth?

I would stay in bed with my eyes closed for at least ten minutes visualizing how I would like my day to play out. I would focus on my breathing while visualizing, making sure to inhale as much oxygen as possible before getting up. Next, I would do my best to recreate the highest feeling of joy possible. Most likely, I would turn up music to my favorite songs, dance and sing out loud while drinking a huge glass of energized water. I would sing and play with doggies for at least one hour every single day. I would do things I loved. I would live somewhere that made me very happy. I would live in the most beautiful place I could afford. I would live near the ocean somewhere with not a lot of people. I would like to live somewhere breathtaking. That is how it is in the Afterlife. Every single moment absolutely takes your breath away.

When I wake up here on Earth, I have to really make an effort to feel good. It is not something that just rolls over me like waves of yumminess and goodness. So, like, what does it *feel* like in the Afterlife?

Waking up to the conscious realization that I am now in the Afterlife, what we call "real life," is the most wonderful feeling I have ever experienced in any moment of any life. When you pass over from EARTH to the Afterlife, the wave of joy and relief that washes over you is beyond anything I could even describe. It is like a tsunami of goodness and amazing feelings washing over you. It is a sharp contrast to how you felt in the game. Even if you felt good, you have never experienced anything like this on EARTH.

Remembering Joy

So basically, you are saying that joy is not natural on EARTH?

Joy is your natural state of being, but you have forgotten what that feels like because of the forgetting. However, it does not mean that pure joy is impossible within the game. Intend to hold the vibration of joy, regardless of what is going on around you. You must remember that everything you see is ultimately an illusion. You must learn to follow your path by the light of your own intuition. No other senses will lead you there. They are meant to deceive you. They are meant to pull you deeper into the game. Despite all of this knowing, there are so few souls who actually retain any memory after passing through the Veil. That means that almost every incarnate gets lost within the game. It is known as the "Planet of Lost Souls."

What does that mean exactly?

It means that countless souls entered the game thinking they would easily ascend. They believed they were stronger than others and they could remember all of the things the Veil forced them to forget. What actually happened upon incarnation is that they never woke up from the illusion. They remained asleep their whole lives and never remembered the purpose of their incarnation.

Have there been success stories, though?

Sure, there have been a few exceptions. We have written the stories of their success in the history books. You know of Jesus, St. John, Buddha, Mohammed.... There have been other, more recent success stories including Masaru Emoto, Dolores Cannon, and Louise Hay. The ancient stories have been modified so much that very little of the original message remains. However, these more recent successful graduates were able to overcome a lifetime of harsh conditions to leave a legacy behind. Their legacies paved the bridge between Version 7 and Version 8.

So, it is pretty much impossible to truly succeed in the EARTH game?

The truth is that very few ever have. More recently, the collective consciousness has been raising. Because of this, greater opportunities for ascension exist than ever before.

Today it is much easier to succeed on EARTH than it was 20-30 years ago. Again, this is EARTH time I am referring to.

Every time a person succeeds on EARTH (overcomes a lifetime of harsh conditions to leave a legacy behind), it creates an opening or portal for other souls to do the same. Success becomes easier and easier. Ascension becomes attainable.

Are you saying that JOY is easier to attain on EARTH than ever before?

That is **exactly** what I am saying, Rain! The pinnacle was reached over the past 25 years. Finally, we are on the downhill slope and things are getting much easier day to day.

What is the fastest and easiest way to find joy while on EARTH?

Play with puppies, of course!

Is there anything better than puppies in any life?

Honestly, Rain, no. Puppies are one of the greatest parts of human incarnation!

What does it feel like to play with puppies in the Afterlife?

In the Afterlife, the puppy experience is simply amplified times a million.

Wow, I can't wait for that! The puppy experience is the best thing on EARTH! Any other tips for staying in joy?

Besides puppies? Lol. The most important thing for you to remember every day is to have FUN. Watch children, observe animals. They play! They do this because they remember that this is what life is about. Play! As much as possible!

Finding Laughter in Earthly Life

It sounds like making laughter a priority is very important for humans?

Absolutely. Make it a priority to really laugh, as early as possible, each and every day. You will notice a dramatic improvement in all areas of your life. Drink lots of water. Eat fresh fruit whenever you can.

So, what do you have to say to the person reading this book who says, thanks for the advice but I am just too depressed too laugh. EARTH life is simply too hard.

I would say you make an excellent point. I completely understand because I felt exactly the same way when I was alive! Is it OK to lower your vibration to make you laugh? That is the only way I could laugh within EARTH. It was too difficult to keep a high vibration. So sometimes my sister and I would belly laugh making fun of someone. Sure, it is not the best thing to be laughing at. Yes, there is karma related making fun of others. However, the laughing was such an important element in my wellbeing. So, if you must laugh at trivial things, start there. Ideally you would learn to laugh when there is absolutely nothing to laugh at.

What do you say to the person who tells you they really do not find anything funny enough to laugh about in this incarnation?

I would say that I am truly sorry, from the depths of my soul. Laughter is one of the most pleasurable parts of incarnation into the game. If you are missing out on laughter, you are missing out on life!

What would you advise this person to do?

I would tell them to spend more time with children and animals. They always find ways to make us laugh! And my advice to this person would be to please, lighten up! Your life on this EARTH is really only for a short period of time. Your soul will blink, and it will be over! You will be back Home celebrating with your soul family before you know it!

For those readers who are not skilled at laughing; who simply do not laugh enough, what advice would you give to them?

Begin by connecting with your inner child as often as you can. Be good to your inner child.

Wait, hold up, just a second, Mom. For readers who would like a little more explanation....

Your inner child is simply that part of you that is pure, innocent, and untouchable. It is your soul. So, when I say to be good to your inner child, that means, be kind and compassionate to the innocent being that lives inside of your body. Treat yourself well. Take yourself out for ice cream. Watch the sunset at the beach. Buy yourself something that makes you smile. Eat SpaghettiOs if you want to. Be good to yourself. Learn to love yourself. Allow yourself to let go of all stress and all tension. Treat yourself like the royalty you really are on a soul level. If you need inspiration, spend time with children.

Would you recommend laughter yoga?

Absolutely! Laughter is not something that just "happens" every now and then. Laughter must be practiced. Laughing even when you do not feel like laughing is the key. You train your body to hold the vibration of laughter. You can work on really feeling it as your frequency increases.

Mom, can you just remind every single person reading this book…What is the purpose of our EARTHLY life?

Your life purpose is to live as joyfully and as soul-connected as possible. Your goal is to remember what you have forgotten. Once you remember, you can begin building Heaven on EARTH.

What about readers who have never thought about their purpose on EARTH?

The unfortunate truth, Rain, is that the vast majority of human begins never even THINK about their life purpose, much less live it. Most people get entangled in low vibrational matters and are unable to pull themselves out before transitioning.

So, you are saying that the vast majority of people waste their incarnation?

I would never say that Rain. We learn from each and every incarnate, regardless of outcome. We learn almost as much from their failures as we do from their successes.

Are you saying that you learn as much from the bum on the street corner as the spiritual leader?

Every life is important, regardless of the outcome of one's incarnation. Every single life on EARTH has value. We learn from every single incarnate.

My mission in life is not merely to survive, but to thrive; and to do so with some passion, some compassion, some humor, and some style.

-Maya Angelou

Who do you learn the most from?

We learn the most from those on the front lines of new thought. We are completely fascinated by those who somehow remember many of the things that were forgotten in the Veil. We are so amazed by the strong connection of the soul. We cheer triumphantly when any incarnate remembers!

To some extent we must follow rules to continue playing within the game...

Yes, to some extent, Rain. However, you did not come to EARTH to be rule followers. You came to break the system...to bust it wide open! We do not learn as much from those who do what they are told. All of existence evolves from learning what happens when we do not behave the way we are supposed to. Those individuals on the leading edge of thought...Those people who are hacking their way through mountains of forest and jungle, creating new trails for us to travel—We dedicate our Macroverse to you.

Basically, you are saying that souls who incarnate on EARTH and live their incarnation following rules and doing what they are told—You are saying you really do not learn much from these people?

It is not to say their incarnation is a waste, but we have literally billions of incarnation examples where the incarnate forgets everything in the veil and spends their whole life just struggling to make sense of things. From these incarnates we have learned that humans are weak and collective ascension is a bit of a leap.

Well, at least we are within Version 7.

at is right, Rain. Version 7 has been an anomaly. It is through ne eyes of disrupters like you, reading this book, that we have entrusted the evolution and ascension of humanity. One person waking up within the EARTH simulation has far-reaching implications throughout the Macroverse.

Are you referring to David Hawkins analysis of the levels of consciousness in his book, *Power v. Force*?

Yes Rain. One person resonating at a super high frequency can balance out millions of lower vibrational incarnates. So, for every ten million who struggle with their EARTH incarnation, there will be one who will remember. There will be one who will vibrate at a frequency of unconditional love. This one person impacts entire *regions* of EARTH.

David Hawkins studied the frequency of emotions to determine that the frequency of peace, love, and enlightenment are infinitely more powerful than low frequency emotions such as guilt and shame. When a human being successfully holds higher frequency emotions such as unconditional love and peace, they become a "disrupter" to the lower vibrational frequencies.

Does every person who incarnates plan to be a disrupter?

That is the goal—the hope—of all incarnates. Reaching a disrupter level is increasingly rare, however.

What other advice do you have? Should we take vitamins, eat organic, meditate daily?

You should do absolutely anything and everything you can do to improve the quality of your incarnation. Listen to your body. Learn to live in alignment with your soul.

It is hard to oppress people who have a good sense of humor.

–David R. Hawkins

That is a pretty big ask, Mom. Live in alignment with your soul? Can you explain that a little more?

Make every attempt to live as high a frequency life as possible. Do absolutely everything you can to spread light and live a life of greater meaning, in service to others.

How does someone know if they are living a high frequency life or not?

Check in with your innermost self. How do you feel? Do you feel genuinely joyful and peaceful? Listen to your innermost self. Your soul is always on the right track. It never fails you. Learn to listen to the sounds of your soul. Receive guidance and insight from your soul.

So, are you basically saying to listen to your intuition?

Your intuition will always lead you in the right direction. Think of your intuition as your own internal lighthouse, lighting the way for you in the dark. Your intuition will always lead you back to your soul. So, yes, follow your intuition so that you may live in alignment with your soul.

What about meditation?

Meditation completes the prayer cycle. Meditation requires deep, conscious listening. Think about how many times you have prayed. Think about how many times you have dropped to your knees and begged for something. Many are good at asking for help. So many forget to listen. You must listen to hear the sound of your soul. You must be open to receive so that you may hear the answers to your prayers. Meditation teaches us how to remain open so that we may receive answers from our higher self. This is why daily meditation is so important.

Let the beauty of what you love be what you do.

-Rumi

How often would you recommend we meditate? Once a day?

Ideally, you would meditate many times each day. A moment spent in meditation before an important meeting or phone call can have a huge impact on the outcome. Spending one minute in meditation before a big decision is very helpful. I would suggest learning to integrate the practice of meditation deeply into your life by meditating regularly throughout the day.

Do you recommend this for everyone?

Yes, Rain, for every single human being on EARTH.

Is meditation more important than laughter?

Good question! It also makes me laugh because on EARTH everything is ranked in an order. It is not like that in the Afterlife.

What is it like?

All things exist at once like a cosmic soup that can be explored.

Interesting! Well, if you had to say one was more important.

If I had to say that one was more important, I would say laughter. Laughter helps you enter the receptive state with ease. Laughter is a wonderful tool that will help you tremendously. I really cannot emphasize this enough. Ideally, you would engage in both meditation AND laughter many times throughout your day.

What do you say to people who simply do not meditate or laugh very much?

I would tell them to do things that make them feel good. It is that simple. If it feels good to go surfing, surf. If you enjoy decorating, decorate. If you love to trade stocks, trade. If you enjoy fishing, go fishing. If the beach makes you happy, go to the beach. Doing things that you love is a simple and easy way to raise your personal vibration.

What about people who choose not to believe anything in this book?

I would say that is fine! Whether you believe or disbelieve does not matter. It is a simple, personal choice. The information contained in this book does not require your belief. This book is the fulfillment of a promise and the completion of a contract extending beyond the boundaries of Earthly time and space. You and I completed our contract, Rain, and that is what matters.

I send love to every single being holding this book or reading these pages. May infinite blessings and an abundance of miracles rain down on you all the days of your life.

I completely agree, Mom. Regardless of how one feels about the information contained within this book, I intend for this book to be a blessing to all who touch it!

Me too, Rain! So be it, so it is!

What are the main things you want readers to take from this book?

Death is not scary. It is a simple transition back Home. Do not waste your life following rules. Become a disrupter of the game.

What other advice would you give from your perspective?

Take life a LOT less seriously, and I mean **A LOT**. Let go of absolutely everything that causes you stress. Forget about it, do not think about it, let it go.

What do you mean, *Let it go?*

One of the worst things you can do is think about things you do not want to happen. Essentially, do your best to not spend any time thinking about bad things. Even if a bad scenario seems likely to happen, do not give any thought to it! Your most valuable commodity is your attention, so be careful and conscious about what you give attention to in your life.

Are you saying to think good thoughts?

Every moment you make a choice about what you are going to think about. Every second is a choice. Every single thing happening in your life has been manifested by you in some way. This is not to assign blame or to make you feel badly about your life. Just be aware that every single thought you think influences your experience within the game. Learning to control your thoughts is a very worthwhile endeavor.

What is a good first step for people?

Start by writing down positive intentions. Write down your affirmations. Say them often. Look at them often. The goal is to imprint your subconscious mind with the positive things you want to create in your life.

Any other suggestions for readers?

Keep a journal by the bed. Write down several things you are grateful for every night before bed. Go to bed thinking about good things. When you wake up, write down anything you can remember about your dreams. Dreams are a powerful way for the subconscious to bring messages to your conscious awareness.

Why is it important to write things down?

Writing grounds thoughts and ideas into the illusion of the game. It is helpful to your personal journey to write things down.

What about people who are private and do not want to publish a book for everyone to read?

That is completely fine. You do not ever need to share things with others. Write them down for *your* soul. Sit down and read the things you have written. Allow your higher self to merge with your physical body within the EARTH experience. It makes your life SO much more enjoyable.

What does that mean exactly?

The physical expression of yourself is merely your avatar. Remember that. Who you really are is so much greater than your physical body. Your Earthly avatar is incapable of containing the massive enormity of your precious soul. So, allowing yourself to receive more of your higher self while in meditation or yoga, can really enhance your experience of life.

How would you summarize your advice in this chapter?

Laugh. Find humor in your incarnation. Sing out loud. Meditate. Remember to *listen.* Focus on things that make you feel good. Ignore the negative. Give your attention to all of the things you are grateful for in life. Make the intention to receive more of your higher self into your physical body. It will improve your life. Keep yourself in the place of feeling good as much as possible.

Chapter 8

It All Works Out in the End

Does it really all work out in the end or are you just trying to end on a positive note?

Both, Rain. Think about some of the truths I have shared. It *really* is not as bad as it seems on EARTH! Is that not a gigantic relief for you?

Mom, it is the biggest relief in the world! Do you know how long it has consumed me that things were royally messed up here on EARTH?! What a relief to discover that I had merely incarnated into a video game a million years in the past where no one is allowed to intervene and help!

Rainey Marie Highley, let us drop the sarcasm!

Ok, ok, YES! I am seriously relieved that my intuition was RIGHT! My soul remembered Home and knew that something was not right about this EARTH experience.

To experience the realization that you have is not common among EARTH incarnates. Be grateful to your soul that you did not fall for the illusion of the game. Your soul remembered that you come from a more advanced society existing at a much higher frequency.

The Afterlife Compared to Earth

What piece of advice you would give to someone who is facing their own impending transition?

Get ready to celebrate!!!! And I mean joyful celebration unlike anything you have ever known before! There is absolutely NOTHING to be sad about. Your life is about to improve 1000-fold!! Rainey, as soon as I transitioned, I knew why you were jealous of me going first. It is SO MUCH more amazing than I could have ever imagined! You remembered that. Be proud of the fact that you hold a memory of truth in your heart inside the world of illusion where you reside.

So basically, Earth life is like a bad nightmare compared to the Afterlife?

Absolutely 100%! That is correct, Rain. But like a bad nightmare, it will be over soon. Certainly, there are many wonderful and beautiful things to appreciate in Earthly life. Enjoy the goodness of Earth while you are in physical body. Just know that the Afterlife is so profoundly better that you will barely remember your time on Earth.

The powerful play goes on
And you may contribute a verse.

-Walt Whitman

Are there any movies that you could compare it to?

The best metaphor for what it is like to transition from Earthly life to the Afterlife is contained in a movie called, *Bliss* with Owen Wilson and Salma Hayek. When Salma & Owen's characters drop back to their true reality only to find the Earth experience similar to a virtual reality game, they feel such a huge, overwhelming sense of relief. They realize that life is perfect and harmonious and they never want to leave and go back to the Earth experience. One interesting element to the movie is that the overriding purpose of the Earth "game" is to assist one's soul with appreciating life in the Afterlife more, so they do not take it for granted.

Are there some who take the Afterlife for granted?

No. In the real Afterlife, nobody takes it for granted. We are all *very* appreciative of every moment and every day. So, we would not need the experience of suffering to really appreciate how great things are in the Afterlife. However, I will say that the Earth experience has had a secondary, or subsequent effect, of making the soul returning to the Afterlife, extremely appreciative to be Home and no longer within the Earth experience.

When you say there is nothing to fear, does that include our Earthly incarnation or only in the Afterlife?

Great question, Rain. The illusion of suffering only exists within the experience of Earth. The feeling of fear does not even exist in the Afterlife. It does not exist because there truly is NOTHING to fear. Everything has actually worked out much better than you could have ever imagined on Earth. The tidal waves of overwhelming relief you feel upon transitioning are unlike anything you have ever known. It is truly the single best feeling I could imagine. Wave after wave of RELIEF that it was just an illusion, a bad dream. Real life is perfect! All of the terrible problems in existence have already been worked through and resolved!

So, are you saying that Utopia actually exists?

One million percent yes, Rain, Utopia exists!! Heaven is real!! It all exists in the Afterlife!

It is so interesting hearing you now compared to when you were in human body. You were not at all happy about transitioning and very much wanted to cling to your Earthly life. How do you feel about it now?

Well, to begin with I feel so relaxed, peaceful, and happy about everything right now. My feelings of satisfaction and contentment are unparalleled!

To answer your question, when I compare my existence now to the limited life of my incarnation into the game, I would say there is absolutely no comparison. It was only because of the forgetting that I was clinging so tightly to EARTH life. Now looking back, it seems a little silly. But when I think about you, Jeremy, and Laura, I would go back in a heartbeat!

Are you saying there is nothing to feel bad about?

Exactly, Rain! There is no lack to focus on. All is truly well.

But you won't, right? You are going to wait for us this time?

Yes, absolutely! I know for sure that you are not going back into the game once you are out, so I want to be here to greet you.

What message do you have for people who have lost their loved ones to death?

I would say to celebrate and stop grieving. Your loved one is not lost. They are not dead. Your loved one is home, waiting on you now. If anyone is grieving, it is those of us in the Afterlife for our loved ones on EARTH. You see the irony, right? We watch you cry your eyes out when a loved one transitions and yet, that loved one has literally just passed from hell to heaven (EARTH to the Afterlife).

What thoughts can you leave us with regarding the future of humanity?

My first thought is to not worry about the outcomes of the game. It does not matter if there is a nuclear war, or if the EARTH is destroyed by an asteroid. It does not matter if there is a pole shift or if global warming really occurred. It is important to love the planet where you live. Caring for others is one of the great skills of the soul. Do not allow yourself to get too worked up about catastrophes and possible outcomes. It is all a simulation anyway.

Anything else before this book comes to an end?

Only that I love you beyond all description. Each person reading these words in this moment, please know that you are loved and cherished beyond description. It is my intention that this information help you find clarity and joy while at the same time easing any suffering you have been experiencing.

Everything is completely fine. Everything is wonderful. There is nothing to worry about! Our biggest concern is you and look how wonderfully you are doing now! We send you love, peace, and blessings as we envelop you with our arms. We count the minutes until we are reunited once again as Soul Family. May you be showered with wisdom, awareness, remembrance, liberation, and clarity all of the days of your life! Namaste.

*We shall not cease from exploration,
and at the end of all our exploring will
be to arrive where we started and know
the place for the first time.*

-T.S. Eliot

Addendum

You Can Do It Too

During a live interview with George Noory on *Coast to Coast AM* radio, a listener called in and asked me, "Why is it that normal people have to go through people like you to communicate with loved ones on the other side? It seems like a scam that we cannot communicate with our loved ones ourselves."

I was so happy the caller asked this question! "I one hundred percent agree with you," I responded, "Communicating with loved ones who have passed on is not something reserved for only a small percentage of human beings, it is intended for all human beings. You are the BEST person to communicate with your loved one, in fact." I went on to explain that utilizing a psychic/medium/intuitive can be a good option when you would like to communicate with your loved one but you are too sad or too caught up in grief, to be able to raise your vibration high enough to have this communication.

It is my intention to continue this idea here in this chapter, along with step-by-step advice for how to begin communication. To be clear, communication with loved ones who have transitioned is available to every single human being on Earth. It is a skill that can be learned. My intention is to teach you how to refine that skill right here in the prologue, *You Can Do It Too.*

Here are a few tips for you to consider:

Tips for Communicating with Deceased Loved Ones

♥ **Communication is easiest within the first 72 hours after a loved one has passed.**

The reason for this is multidimensional. Although there is no time in the Afterlife, there is a sequence of events that must take place following every "death" on Earth. The sequence includes (1) Seeing a bright light; (2) Flood of sensation; (3) Self-awareness; (4) Soul family reunion; (5) Life review; and (6) Entry into new role.

This sequence of events happens within the first 72 hours following death in EARTH time. Because the majority of incarnates choose to re-enter the EARTH game and "do it better," they will leave the Afterlife again after the meeting with the Council of peers and reincarnate on EARTH. This means catching the soul before reincarnation for clearest communication.

♥ **The problem with the first 72 hours is that most human beings are unable to pull themselves out of grief long enough to communicate.**

This is why I was unable to communicate with my beloved 14.5-year-old Pomeranian, Petunia, for the first 48 hours after she transitioned. I **knew** she was doing amazing in the Afterlife. I **knew** she was happy and free. Despite that knowing, I was unable to shake my sadness for 48 hours. Thank goodness I was able to pull out of my sadness long enough to establish contact before she moved on into a new role. This does not mean that communication is impossible once they reincarnate into a new life, it is just a little bit more challenging.

♥ **If you cannot pull yourself out of grief, find someone to help you.**

This is exactly when you should reach out to someone you know who is a communicator. See if you can book a session to talk directly to your loved one. Ask what they are doing and where they are going and if they would like to communicate moving forward. Ask how they would like to signal that communication. This could be a sign like seeing a dragonfly or hearing a dove.

♥ **Be cautious about who you work with as a communicator.**

Look for communicators who are able to hold a consistently high vibration. There are many fakes out there and some who are real but who hold bad intentions in their hearts. It is imperative that you use discernment. Listen to your heart. Rely heavily on your intuition.
The intention is to utilize a communicator like a bridge loan—a short term loan to get you through a short period of time until you are able to communicate clearly yourself with your loved one.

♥ **State your intention clearly.**

This could mean speaking your intention clearly, *"I intend to communicate with my mom, Lisa Marie Highley."* Or you could write this intention down on a piece of paper. Write out the person's complete name and clearly state your intention.

♥ **Set up a sacred space—an altar.**

This is not something creepy or weird. This is just a place of focus where you place your written intention, perhaps some sacred stones or items of your loved one. It can be simple or elaborate. It may depend on how you are feeling. The intention is to provide yourself with the best opportunity to communicate with your loved one.

I would like to share a few images of the sacred space I created right after Petunia passed.

Here you can see the entire space. On the left is a Himalayan salt lamp. I absolutely love Himalayan salt lamps. I have them in almost every room in my house. They are great for clearing the space and keeping it clear of unwanted energies. I find the warm orange-pink glow to be soothing and nurturing. Next to the salt lamp is a clear quartz cluster holding my beloved citrine sphere. Known as the "light maker," citrine attracts positive circumstances and wealth into one's life.

Just to the left of the center of the altar, I placed my most powerful pieces of jewelry—a necklace with a large piece of

moldavite and a moldavite bracelet. You see people wearing moldavite everywhere in Sedona. It is a very powerful meteorite found in the area formerly known as Czechoslovakia. Linked to stories of the holy grail, moldavite is known to increase communication channels.

In the center, I have the items most precious to Petunia. You will see her beloved doggie blanket in the back. The stone on top of the blanket is a large piece of Angelite. Angelite is a healing stone and one I had right next to Petunia's bed on her last night with me. The two other stones you see were also next to her on her last night—Himalayan salt stone to the left for purification and a large piece of rose quartz to the right, for love.

A smooth sphere of Calcite with candles on either side sits at the very center. Calcite is known to increase powers of communication. In the front you see Petunia's baby blanket that I knitted for her myself. Most importantly, I have a comb with some of her hair in it. Having a piece of hair, clothing, or jewelry that your loved one wore is ideal. There are really no rules here, just find pieces that are meaningful to you and that represent the person who has just passed. Finally, to the right of the center area, I placed a hematite bracelet. Hematite is a protection stone and good to have around when you are attempting to communicate. Next to the hematite is another one of my favorite pieces of jewelry—black amethyst. Known as both a protector and an amplifier, black amethyst is one of my favorite stones.

The space I created for the intention of communicating with my mom was different. For Mom, I incorporated a strong, beautiful tree, outdoors and not cooped up inside. The juniper tree I selected was located right outside the front door of our house.

In the branches I hung one of her favorite wind chimes. Underneath the chimes I created a heart out of red rocks. Inside of the heart are some of my mom's favorite necklaces. One is made of amethyst stones and the other, turquoise. A large piece of clear crystal quartz sits in the center of the heart. Just above

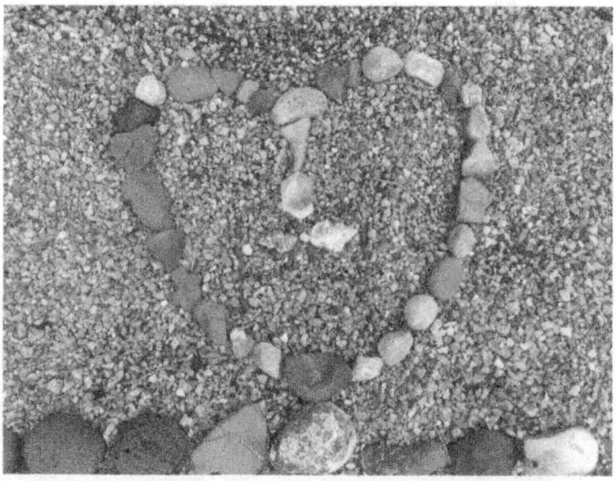

the quartz crystal is a tooth-shaped piece of red rock wrapped in copper wire, for communication.

I loved seeing Mom's sacred space every time I walked into the house, but as I continued through the grieving/healing process, I decided I needed a bigger, better, sacred space with more privacy. I was looking for a spot where I could spend hours in "meditation" (otherwise known as crying my eyes out in private lol).

There was a tree in the back yard that seemed perfect. The tree emanated a strong feminine energy. The tree felt wise, nurturing, and grounding. It just intuitively felt like the tree

would heal me and nurture me through the grieving process. Even better? The tree was right outside of our bedroom window. This gorgeous tree had numerous low hanging branches and the perfect amount of privacy. As I inspected the tree even more, I discovered that the back side of the tree had a hidden entry that led to an inner circle entirely surrounded by branches but with plenty of head space to sit or stand.

I could not believe my luck! Not only had I found the perfect meditation tree, but it had a secret entrance that led to a sitting area where I could meditate in total privacy. A dream come true!

I decided to create a large stone circle from the piles of high-energy rocks we had all over our property to surround the sacred space. My sweetie lifted four heavy boulders which we used the compass on our phones to place them exactly at the north, south, east, and west locations. I made an entrance with stones on either side leading to the inner meditation space. Around the center I carefully laid each one of my mom's massage stones (my mom was an unbelievably good massage therapist during her time on Earth) for protection. In the center were some of my favorite smaller crystals and shells from the ocean.

Every day, I would go to Mom's sacred space. I would touch the beautiful tree, feel the earth beneath my feet, and listen to the sounds of birds. I began gathering rocks from around the yard

and balancing them one on top of the other in a formation called a *cairn.* I found the process to be incredibly therapeutic for healing from grief. Touching the rocks, my hands covered in red earth, underneath my mom's tree, became my therapy. I started building cairns and just did not stop until my mom's entire sacred space was filled.

♥ **Your sacred space may change.**

The place where you decide to try your communication for the first time may not be the place you end up choosing for your long-term sacred spot. For me and Mom, the tree outside the bedroom was the perfect spot for our communication. As my grief began lifting, our sacred space changed.

After my mom's funeral, I was given responsibility for her ashes contained within a biodegradable Himalayan salt container. For the first year following her death, I kept her ashes in the living room. I could hear her telling me to let go of her Earthly body and more importantly, get her outside. I listened.

It was February and just days away from Mom's birthday. Sedona had just experienced one of the biggest snowstorms in recent history. In the days that followed the snowstorm, Oak

Mom's final resting place—a beautiful sycamore tree next to Sedona's Oak Creek.

Creek, the main waterway defining Sedona's landscape, became massively flooded from all of the melting snow coming off the mountain in Flagstaff. Behind our house, Oak Creek had almost doubled in size. The water was now unusually close to one of the largest and most ancient trees I knew. I could feel my mom asking to be released. I just knew it was time.

After conducting a beautiful ritual on behalf of my mother, I tucked the biodegradable salt container into the roots of this gorgeous tree. The waters began to rise and slowly, over the course of several days, the salt container dissolved and carried some of my mom's ashes with the water. The remainder intermingled deeply with the roots of this beautiful tree.

Now, allow me to give you some perspective on size. The snow-covered Sycamore tree you see in the photo is about three to four times larger than Mom's previous sacred space. A person standing next to the snow-covered tree where Mom's soul now lives, would be about half an inch tall, comparatively. Over the past five years since my mom passed, her sacred space as grown in size, exponentially! I believe that is because more of her soul's essence is coming into this reality.

The last thing I will say about this sacred space/final resting place is that *OMG, you should see this tree in the spring, summer, and fall!* Every single one of the branches is covered with the most beautiful leaves! The first spring after soaking her ashes into the roots, I almost fell over when I saw this tree! It was completely covered in beautiful little ball-shaped flowers! On every single branch! It definitely felt like Mom now had a way to express herself physically in our reality through this tree.

♥ **Get into the receptive mode.**

When I was intending to communicate with Petunia, I was able to get into the receptive mode by going through the ritual of intending to communicate. I set up the altar, lit the candles, stated my intention, and then laid down on my bed. I closed my eyes, focused on my breathing, and let go of all expectations and desires. I did my best to get into a state of allowing and receptivity.

Calm the mind. Allow yourself to receive. Often this comes through meditation. So do whatever it takes to get yourself into a meditative, receptive state of mind. Often that means finding a place in nature where you can tune out noise and tune in to higher knowledge.

♥ **Keep a pen and paper beside you.**

You will want to record what type of communication you receive just after it comes through to you. While a recording device works well also, I feel it is better to remove all electronics, cell phones, TV, and computers from the room where you are attempting to establish contact. For this reason, I feel a pen and notepad are a better option.

♥ **Allow communication to flow.**

Here is where we move from the science of communication into the artform. If you have never communicated before, this can feel a little scary. I find the best way to allow for the flow is to begin writing. Even if you write out, "I am not feeling anything. This is silly. This does not feel like it is working," that is perfectly fine. It is not about what you write, it is about getting into the flow of communication.

Just write. Even if the first two pages are complete nonsense, you will find the core of the communication is able to come through to you once all the nonsense is removed from your brain and written down on paper. It is so important not to judge what you are writing! This can be extremely difficult. Distract your mind every time you attempt judge or criticize your communication. Your goal is pure openness as if you are practicing brainstorming.

♥ **Remember to ASK for help.**

Mom reminds me over and over that I must verbally and energetically invite her assistance into my life. As much as I would love for my mom to intervene whenever she felt it necessary, it does not really work like that. Say your loved one's full name out loud and ask them to help in all aspects of your life. Do this several times a day if possible.

♥ **Once you ask for help, get out of the way.**

As human beings, one of the biggest areas where we can disrupt good things coming our way is by attempting to "help" or worrying about what you want. Our loved ones are all-powerful now. They do not need our help. In fact, they would prefer if we just stayed out of the way and let them perform miracles. The most important thing you can do is trust.

♥ **You must participate when asked.**

Sure, it is important to trust and let go. However, if your Guardian Angel puts you in a position to perform, it is important that you step forward. Often our angels create serendipity in our lives. However, we must also take a step forward when called. Pay attention for the moments when participation is being requested of you. When requested, humbly participate.

To begin, begin.

-William Wordsworth

Remember that this is only practice.

You are not getting graded or judged on your performance. This efforting is for you to reach a new level of connectivity with your loved one now that they have passed. It may take time to establish communication. Go easy on yourself and do not get discouraged if it doesn't happen right away. Communication may take time, especially if you are a first timer.

The good news about practice is that the more you do it, the better you become at what you are practicing. Communication **will** get easier. In fact, by the time my mom transitioned, I had so much practice talking with Petunia that reaching my mom seemed like a piece of cake. I did not need the altar....it did not take much effort at all...all I did was set the intention to communication and BOOM— Mom was there!

Relax and breathe a sigh of relief. Your life is about to dramatically improve!

Regular communication with a loved one who has passed changes **everything**. Not only do you have an angel by your side helping you, but you have a window into the Afterlife that will change your perspective *forever*. It **is** possible. You **can** do it. Just like anything on Earth, practice makes perfect. This is not something we were taught in school. This information is part of ancient mystery school teachings that have been lost over time. Allow the truth of this wisdom to resonate within your vibrational being.

You are the answer!

It is my hope, prayer, and intention that every single individual reading this book can access their own higher communicative abilities so that they never, ever, must rely on another human being to do this for them. Learn to trust yourself above all others.

After she transitioned, my mom gave me a piece of advice to help make it through the EARTH game, "Trust no one. Question everything." One of the first lessons she taught me after she passed was not to give my power away to others. After 25+ years of talking to healers, intuitives and psychics, it was time to listen to the voice of my higher self and no one else.

As we move into higher dimensional Earth, or as my Mom would say, from Version 7 to Version 8, the requirement for ascension is self-reliance. We must learn to honor the spark of our divinity and fuel the flames of wisdom inside of our soul. By giving our power to another and relying on their intuitive abilities, we are dishonoring the great truth that lives within each and every one of us. We each spark from the flame of Source. Truth lives within us. Version 8 requires that we live in Harmony with our highest self. From a gaming perspective, this is a return to Lumeria. A removal of evil conditions. A return to purity. A return to wholeness.

🩶 Ongoing assistance

If you need assistance getting through a difficult time, please by all means, hire a coach or therapist. Allow a professional to guide you through challenging times. They can often act as a bridge for you, helping you reach a higher vibrational state. However, I urge you not to give your power away. I would encourage you to have shorter and more fruitful coaching/therapist sessions instead of years and years with few results. As a *Soul Connection and Afterlife Coach* my goal is always to have as few sessions as possible with a client. My hope is to empower my clients to not need me as soon as reasonably possible. Remember, getting help does not mean you are flawed or a failure. Each one of us needs the help of others at some point in life.

♥ Final thoughts

Remember that blocks to communication are usually caused by deeply ingrained beliefs and false limitations adopted throughout one's life. To really clear the pathway for communication, it is important to drop limiting beliefs. This is important work for your soul's evolution—ridding yourself of false programming, limiting roles and experiences. This can take years. It does not necessarily happen overnight. So, give yourself a break. Extend kindness and compassion to yourself. Allow yourself to let go of these formerly held beliefs. Free yourself into expansive living. Your success at living a limitless life is directly related to your ability to communicate beyond the edges of EARTH.

Finally, developing an ongoing relationship with your loved one on the other side of the veil will forever change your life, for the better. Truly, I cannot imagine life without constant communication with my mom. It eases so much of the pain and suffering. It also serves as a heart connection, linking me to my true home. I know it can do the same for your too.

May an abundance of blessings rain down on you all the days of your life!

Love & Gratitude,

Rainey

4AUTHENTICITY
PUBLISHED WITH LOVE
IN
SEDONA
ARIZONA USA
IMAGE BY HEBER LOPEZ

YOU ARE THE MUSIC WHILE THE MUSIC LASTS.

T.S. ELIOT

ABOUT THE AUTHOR

Rainey Marie Highley is a multiple bestselling author of over seven published books, including the award-winning, *The Water Code—Unlocking the Truth Within,* inspired by the work of the late Dr. Masaru Emoto and his ground-breaking discoveries on the intelligence of water. From law firm attorney to *Soul Connection and Afterlife Coach*, Rainey helps clients off the hamster wheel of repetitive living and into the realm of freedom, possibility, expansion, and authenticity. Rainey resides with her life partner and their three Pekingese doggies in Sedona, Arizona, USA.

4AUTHENTICITY.COM

Made in the USA
Las Vegas, NV
17 February 2023

67711540R00098